It All Adds Up!

**Engaging
8-to-12-Year-Olds in
Math
Investigations**

Math Solutions Publications
Sausalito, California

Math Solutions Publications
A division of
Marilyn Burns Education Associates
150 Gate 5 Road, Suite 101
Sausalito, CA 94965
http://www.mathsolutions.com

Library of Congress Cataloging-in-Publication Data
Skinner, Penny.
    It all adds up! : engaging 8-to-12-year-olds in math
investigations / Penny Skinner : foreword by Marilyn Burns.
      p.   cm.
    Previously published: Melbourne : Longman Australia, 1998.
    ISBN 0-941355-24-1 (pbk.)
    1. Arithmetic—Study and teaching (Elementary).   I. Title.
QA115.S56   1999
372.7'2—dc21   99-32410
                                          CIP

Editor: Cynthia Dean
Designer: Lucy Adams
Illustrators: Pat Kermode and Bruce Rankin
Cover designer: Lucy Adams

Set in Minion
Produced by Addison Wesley Longman Australia PTY Limited

Printed in the United States of America
99 00 01 02 03 04 05 06 07 08 10 9 8 7 6 5 4 3 2 1

A Message from Marilyn Burns

We at Marilyn Burns Education Associates believe that teaching mathematics well calls for continually reflecting on and improving one's instructional practice. Our Math Solutions Publications include a wide range of choices, from books that describe problem-solving lessons, to *Math By All Means* units that show how to teach specific topics, to resources that help link math with writing and literature, to children's books that help students develop an appreciation for math while learning basic concepts.

Along with our large collection of teacher resource books, we have a more general collection of books, videotapes, and audiotapes that can help teachers and parents bridge the gap between home and school. All of our materials are available at education stores, from distributors, and through major teacher catalogs.

In addition, Math Solutions Inservice offers five-day courses and one-day workshops throughout the country. We also work in partnership with school districts to help implement and sustain long-term improvement in mathematics instruction in all classrooms.

To find a complete listing of our publications and workshops, please visit our Web site at www.mathsolutions.com. Or contact us by calling (800) 868-9092 or sending an e-mail to info@mathsolutions.com. We'd be pleased to send you a copy of our complimentary Math Solutions Newsletter in which we share teaching ideas, new resources, student work, and information about important issues concerning math education.

We're eager for your feedback and interested in learning about your particular needs. We look forward to hearing from you.

A DIVISION OF MARILYN BURNS EDUCATION ASSOCIATES

To my children, Katie and Jonathan, who taught me so much about how children learn mathematics. Their assertion, "Mum, there's school maths and there's real maths," made we want to do something about changing the way mathematics was taught.

To my teaching partners, Pam Daly and Kathy Bingham, who have shared my excitement in teaching mathematics through problem solving and investigation.

Foreword

Marilyn Burns

When Toby Gordon, the Math Solutions Publications publishing director, first gave me a copy of *It All Adds Up!*, I began reading it eagerly. I was searching for better ways to teach arithmetic, to be able to approach it with the same spirit and excitement I had for the other areas of the mathematics curriculum. I wanted to help students develop arithmetic competence, confidence, and efficiency while also helping them develop their number sense, problem-solving ability, and appreciation for mathematical thinking and reasoning.

I was delighted to discover that the author of this book, Australian teacher Penny Skinner, promised to address my concerns. In the introduction, Penny explains that her book explores teaching strategies for helping students become competent with computation while also developing an enthusiasm for mathematics. She describes how she uses students' interests, problems, and ideas as the basis for her teaching. She writes about the importance of having children work alone and in small groups to gain experience with computation through exploring mathematical topics and solving problems.

I finished the book in a single sitting. Not only did Penny deal with many of the issues I was confronting, her book confirmed my goals and gave me fresh, practical, classroom-tested suggestions to try with my students. I liked the book so much that I arranged with the Australian publisher to make it available through Math Solutions Publications for teachers here in the United States.

Many elements in the book contribute to its being a useful and valuable resource for teachers. It addresses ways to teach addition, subtraction, multiplication, and division, and includes work on whole numbers, fractions, decimals, and percents. Samples of student work illustrate students' responses to the lessons and their different ways of thinking.

Classroom transcripts bring to life how Penny and her teaching partner, Pam Daly, presented many of the lessons. Suggested problem-solving investigations offer ways to engage students in developing mathematical understanding and thinking about computation. And at its heart the book combines two of Penny's deep interests and passions—helping students make sense of mathematics and helping teachers become more effective teachers of mathematics.

Importing books from other countries often requires translation. This isn't an issue with a book from Australia, since it was of course published in English. However, you'll find a few differences in the book's use of language that can be a bit jarring and perhaps off-putting if you're used to reading only "American" English. For example, you'll notice in the table of contents that the section on posing and solving problems addresses "*Organising* Problem Posing" and the section on multiplication includes a "'*Maths* Party' activity" to engage the students with rectangular numbers. In the body of the book, you'll encounter children being given problems to solve "over a *fortnight*," measurements that involve "*metres*," and strategies for helping students "*memorise*," "*visualise*," and "*practise*." While these terms and spellings reflect differences in how English is used over the world, they don't imply differences in how to think about teaching children. Nor do they detract from the commonsense advice the book offers.

A few other clarifications are helpful as well. The book was written for teachers of "middle and upper primary grades." In Australia, "primary school" goes through age twelve. The book addresses mathematics taught to children ages eight through twelve and is appropriate for our grades 3 through 6. When the book refers to "Year 4" students or a "Year 5/6" class, you can safely apply those same numbers to our grade levels. You'll also see large numbers written without commas, so that 27,863, for example, appears as 27 863. And when you see "MAB blocks" referred to in the book, know that these are the same as the base ten blocks available to us here.

Aside from these cosmetic differences, I felt completely at home in Penny Skinner's classroom. I was excited by her ideas and appreciative of the help she gave me in thinking about my own teaching. If you're interested in ways to engage your students with estimation, mental arithmetic, written computation, and mathematical investigations, you'll find this book to be a valuable addition to your teaching resources.

Contents

Introduction   **7**

Working Mathematically   **7**

Computation   **8**

Principles of Mathematics Teaching   **10**

Working through a Syllabus   **12**

    Strategies for encouraging syllabus-related investigations   12

Posing and Solving Problems

Organising Problem Posing   **13**

    Posing problems for middle and upper primary students   13

Posing Problems on Specific Mathematical Topics   **16**

Scaffolding Problem Writing   **18**

Sharing Students' Problems   **19**

Investigating

The Investigation Process   **20**

    Beginning an investigation   20

    The language students use to explain ideas   20

    Writing a definition   21

    Searching for patterns   22

    Posing questions   22

Group Work   **23**

    Establishing working groups   23

    Bringing groups together   23

Report Writing   **24**
    Note making   24
    Making diagrams   26
    Modelling report writing   26

Reviewing an Investigation   **28**

Addition

Single-digit Addition Strategies   **29**

Addition Chains   **33**

Adding Two-digit Numbers   **34**
    Mental addition   34
    Written addition   35
    Spreadsheet addition   39

Addition Practice through Investigations   **40**

Adding Larger Numbers   **42**

Adding Decimals   **43**

Triangular Numbers   **44**

Fibonacci Numbers   **48**

Pascal's Triangle   **49**

Multiplication

Investigating Sequences of Multiples   **51**
    Multiples of nine   51
    Reducing numbers   55
    Multiples of four   55
    Multiples of five and twenty-five   58
    Zero as a multiple   59
    Multiples and angles   62
    Multiples of eight   62
    Common multiples   64

Multiplication Strategies   **66**
    Doubling   66
    Multiplying by single-digit numbers   67
    The standard algorithm   69
    Multiplying by eleven   71
    Multiplying by numbers greater than eleven   74
    Multiples of ninety-nine   78

Square Numbers   **79**
    Square number problems   81
    Square number investigations   84

Rectangular Numbers   **88**
    Factors   89
    Linking factors with square numbers   92
    Linking factors with the binary sequence   94
    Factors and angles   94
    Introducing prime numbers   95
    'Maths Party' activity   96

Measuring Area and Volume   **96**

Cubic Numbers   **97**

Multiplying Decimals   **100**

Permutations and Factorials   **101**

Subtraction

Subtraction Contexts   **105**
    Finding differences   105
    Taking away   106

Single-digit Subtraction Strategies   **106**

Subtracting Larger Numbers   **107**
    Estimation   107
    Mental subtraction   108
    Written subtraction   110

Subtraction Practice through Investigations 112
Negative Numbers 114
Subtracting Decimals 119
Pyramid Numbers 119

Division

Division Contexts **120**
    Fractions 120
    Quotition division 121
    Partition division 121
    Percentages 121
    Multiplication tables 122

Division Strategies **122**
    Dividing by single-digit numbers 122
    Making sense of division answers 126
    Making sense of calculator answers to division 127

Divisibility **129**
    Divisibility by five and ten 129
    Divisibility by other single-digit numbers 130
    Divisibility by eleven 130
    Divisibility by twelve 131

Division with Decimals **132**
    Linking fractions and decimals 133
    Why do some decimals repeat infinitely? 136

Percentages **138**
    Percentage calculation devices 138

Conclusion 140

Posing Questions in View of the Mathematics Teaching Principles 144

Introduction

This book explores effective teaching strategies and mathematical topics that are directed at achieving competence in computation and an enthusiasm for working mathematically in middle and upper primary school students. Reports of teacher and student participation in many lessons involving working with numbers are featured throughout the book.

Working Mathematically

The teaching described in this book targets the development of each child's understandings, knowledge and skills as they work mathematically. 'Working mathematically' children explore mathematical topics and solve problems, developing and applying mathematical techniques as they do so.

Many of the topics and problems in a mathematics classroom can be initiated by the children themselves. In a classroom focused on working mathematically, teachers and children work together as a community of learners; they explore ideas together and share what they find. It is very different to the traditional method of mathematics teaching, which begins with a demonstration by a teacher and continues with children practising what has been demonstrated. The following account illustrates the method of mathematics teaching I have developed and implemented with many classes.

For two years I have teamed with another teacher, Pam Daly, to teach mathematics to middle and upper primary students. Pam and I brought our classes together for a short introduction to each lesson, often drawing on the work of the children to present problems or set a topic for investigation.

The children worked alone or in small groups to produce their lists and search for patterns. When Pam and I joined in with the children as they worked, we monitored each child's progress, noting their understandings, knowledge and skills, and we intervened to help them develop understandings and challenge misconceptions.

The understandings, knowledge and skills we monitored were not only content based, such as: *How does this child carry out addition? What language does this child use to describe what they are doing when they add?* but were also relevant to how the child worked mathematically: *How does this child begin an investigation? How does this child contribute in a group?*

At the end of each lesson, Pam and I gathered our classes separately in different parts of our shared room. Each class wrote up a list of their mathematical explorations or patterns, drawing on what the class as a whole had done. If my class discovered a new pattern I would go across to Pam's class to tell them. This knowledge sharing is how Pam and I modelled our enthusiasm for mathematics and drew the children into the exciting world of mathematical exploration.

Computation

The children involved in the type of investigation described above were gaining experience in computation as they worked. Problems and investigations are important because, not only do they develop children's ability to work mathematically, they also set the context for purposeful computation.

Mental, written and calculator strategies can all be developed and practised through problems and investigations.

- Mental computation is the most important of the three in the primary school years, as it helps develop an understanding of computation processes and is fundamental to competent calculator use.

- Estimation is one of the keys to successful mental calculation. Quite often an estimate is all that is required and mental calculation should be the means of making an estimate. Exact answers should first be estimated, for the purpose of ensuring the final answer makes sense in terms of the problem, then calculated mentally or with calculators or computers.

- One important role of written computation is to assist mental computation. Sometimes it is useful to record subtotals on the way to finding an answer mentally. Standard written algorithms can be useful in helping to understand why certain answers and patterns occur. For example, if eleven multiplied by eleven is calculated in writing it is quite clear why 121 is the answer.

- Calculators are powerful tools for investigating important mathematical ideas, and for assisting students to learn mental and written computation concepts and strategies. For example, if children are learning to use a standard algorithm, they can use a calculator to check their answers. If their answers are correct, they can be confident they are using the algorithm correctly. If their answers are incorrect the calculator answer may help them see where they went wrong.

Principles of Mathematics Teaching

The following principles underpin the approach to teaching mathematics outlined in this book.

1   A mathematics program is concerned essentially with each student's progress as a mathematician.

   Mathematicians are enthused and fascinated by problems, puzzles and patterns. They are competent problem-solvers and investigators who confidently use a variety of skills and draw on a wide range of knowledge.

2   Problems and investigations are central to a mathematics program.

   As students pose and solve problems and investigate mathematical topics, they learn mathematics in a real context so that mathematics makes sense to them. Within the context of problems and investigations, students gain knowledge and skills and apply them purposefully.

3   Teachers use the problems posed by students as starting points for further work.

   Students are very interested in the problems their friends pose and they like to challenge each other with increasingly complex problems. Each student can write problems that draw on their own background experiences and understandings, and this is one way a mathematics program is inclusive of all students.

4   There is no one way to solve a problem; students work out their own ways to find answers.

   With the support of teachers who facilitate learning, rather than directly teaching techniques for working out answers, students can learn a wide range of problem-solving strategies through investigation and experimentation in cooperation with their friends.

5   Students build an understanding of mathematical ideas through many practical investigations and through talking with their teachers and friends about their observations and ideas.

   In mathematics lessons students might be cutting and pasting, drawing and painting, building models, making patterns, playing games and explaining and discussing ideas. Teachers have a major role to play in helping students move from concrete experiences, which they discuss in their own language, to the symbolic expression of mathematical ideas.

6   Teachers primarily use the language the students spontaneously use and gradually introduce them to more sophisticated terminology as they find a need for it.

By using the students' own words, we make a significant contribution to their growing understanding of mathematics and their progress along the path towards symbolic expression. Students should do a lot of talking and writing in mathematics lessons. They discuss their ideas, write problems and write reports on their investigations of mathematical topics. They will learn the standard terminology and symbols of mathematics so that they can communicate mathematical ideas effectively.

7   Teachers help students learn skills and acquire knowledge as outcomes of their work with problems and investigations.

Learning skills and acquiring knowledge should not be ends in themselves, their acquisition should be purposeful. Problem solving and investigation provide a purposeful context.

8   Teachers are particularly concerned that students develop the skills of visualisation, estimation and mental calculation.

These three skills areas, essential to effective problem-solving and investigation, are reciprocally linked with a knowledge of number facts: as students visualise, estimate and mentally calculate, they build a bank of number facts, and as they acquire number fact knowledge, they enhance their ability to work out answers and discover patterns through visualisation, estimation and mental calculation.

9   Teachers monitor each student's progress.

By compiling a profile of each student's growth as a mathematician, using anecdotal records, interview notes and work samples, teachers can monitor each student's progress. Students can be closely involved in monitoring their own progress.

Working through a Syllabus

One possible constraint to adopting a teaching approach based on children's interests, problems and ideas is the need to follow a prescribed syllabus. A syllabus, however, need not constrain mathematics teaching. It can be viewed as a framework for topic selection and a means to extend children's thinking.

Strategies for encouraging syllabus-related investigations

■ List and display set topics of study for the year for children to see on cards pinned around the tops of the walls.

■ Encourage students to become curious about some topics after seeing them listed. 'What's a mixed number? Can we learn about percentages next?'

■ Ask a group of students to research a listed topic and set some problems to introduce it to the rest of the class. Refer students to the list to explain why particular investigation topics are being proposed.

■ When a student poses a problem that relates to a listed topic, draw the class's attention to it and suggest further exploration of that topic.

Posing and Solving Problems

Organising Problem Posing

Throughout the primary school years, problems are central to a mathematics program, particularly problems that students themselves pose. The students' problems may be real or contrived, as long as they are posed in the spirit of mathematical exploration. Children like to challenge each other and test out their new understandings with their problems, and they are usually keen to solve the problems set by their peers. Having students pose problems is also a useful evaluation strategy as, through their problems, they reveal to teachers their mathematical understandings and misconceptions.

Teachers also have a role to play in posing problems, primarily: to model possibilities, ensure students meet a wide range of problem types and focus on understandings, knowledge and skills across a diversity of mathematical topics. There are several ways problem posing can be organised for middle and upper primary students. The following three ways have been successful.

Posing problems for middle and upper primary students

- A Personal Book for writing problems from which they read at a class or group problem sharing time.

- **Cards** which can be filed for use at an appropriate time; the problems can be sorted easily if necessary, as sometimes it is useful to extract a particular concept from a collection of problems.
- Hang Sheets of Paper on a Classroom Wall and ask students to record their problems in a felt-tip pen. The teacher can model writing problems on the paper and suggest to students that they can add problems to the collection.

The following problems appeared in a Year 5/6 class over a fortnight. They were written by the children on a long sheet of paper pinned to the classroom wall. Note the variety and the wealth of starting points for work. Note also the sources of the problems; some students have written problems similar to ones met in previous mathematics classes, some have presented real problems, some have posed problems as an outcome of investigative work and some have been inspired to offer original problems.

I bought a piece of pizza costing 25c for one eighth of the pizza. The whole pizza costs $1.50. Would it be cheaper to buy the whole pizza or one eighth at a time?

If Johnny had 6449 marbles and had to share them amongst 7 people, how many marbles would there be left over?

Sue went shopping and bought a pair of jeans that cost $40.95, 3 Mars Bars that cost 63c each and a present for her Mum that cost $15.62. How much change did she have if she took $65 with her?

If there were 1,080 children in a school, how many staff would the school need?

Look at this pattern:
98-89=9 87-78=9 76-67=9 65-56=9
54-45=9 43-34=9 32-23=9 21-12=9
10-01=9   How can this be?

Try and make more than 235 words on your calculator.

A Swiss skier died when he was practising speed skiing before his Olympic race. The slope was 70% gradient. How many degrees are in the angle at the bottom of the slope?

We are making models of Jupiter and Venus. Jupiter's diameter is 142,800 km and Venus' diameter is 12,100 km. We are using a scale of 1 cm: 2,000 km. How big will our models be? [Another child added the next question.] What about the sun?

1992 is the 16th Winter Olympics. They are on every four years so when were the first ones on? Listen to the TV and see if you are right.

A typical range of real and theoretical problems posed by Year 5/6 students.

Often, when a student poses a type of problem new to their classmates, others respond by posing similar problems or extending the scope of the original problem. Sometimes students engage in an exchange of problems exploring a concept, developing each other's ideas and setting challenges. The following sequence of problems is an example of this. One girl wrote the first problem and, as others found they enjoyed the challenge of working on it, they set the later problems.

What is one fifth of one half?

What is a fifth of a quarter?

What is a third times a third?

What is a tenth of a tenth?

What is a third of a twentieth?

An initial problem often prompts other students to extend the scope of the original investigation.

To add variety to the task of posing problems, a teacher can occasionally ask students to suggest a theme for their problems. Some examples teachers and children have suggested are: animal statistics, sports, Christmas, countries of the world, maps, food, temperatures, holidays and cars.

Another successful exercise is to take students into particular settings, such as the school playground, to search for possible problems. The outdoors has proved to be a rich source of ideas for problems related to school buildings, playground structures, car park statistics, shadow lengths, sports field measurements, playground usage statistics, distances, shape and measurement.

Posing Problems on Specific Mathematical Topics

Teachers can sometimes challenge students to pose problems on a particular mathematical topic. This can be an excellent way to introduce a specific topic of work, sometimes drawn from a set syllabus. For instance, students in one class were asked to write problems involving fractions. After the problems had been written, data was collected on the fractions they had used. Most had posed problems involving half, one-quarter or three-quarters and a few had used thirds. Only one child had used other types of fractions and this fact was the focus of discussion about the most commonly used fractions in real life, and where and when fractions are useful.

Children in a Year 4/5 class wrote the following fraction problems.

Wayne had a problem. He flunked all his tests in maths. On day wayne had a test and his parents told him if he diosdn't pass he would be grounded for five weeks. So wayne worked very hard. He only got one question wrong!!! That question was a sequence question. It went 1/4, 1/2, 3/4 -, -. Well wayne went home and his parents were so pleased with him that they gave him a raise. He had got a A. But wayne never worked out the answer can you?

I saw that there was a cake. I ate half, my friend had half of what was left. How much did my friend have?

I went to the shop to buy 4 cans of baked beans. They only had 3 in stock. What is the fraction I had to get from another shop?

I was sitting in maths one day and I counted 47 holes in my shoe. I told my mum and she fixed it. How many holes did I have left?

There was one megabyte of RAM left on the computer. There are 1 million bytes in one megabyte. There was a program that took up 9 and a quarter megabytes, I took it off. How much memory is there now?

Children typically pose fraction problems involving halves and quarters.

The problem about the holes in the shoe is an example of a 'trick' question, something that arises occasionally and delights the students.

When beginning a study of area, a class of Year 5/6 students was set the task of writing problems about area. This helped the teacher know something of the students' understandings and knowledge about area, and provided some starting points for work. Here are some of the problems that were produced.

Area

In the middle of the Cold War, when the Berlin wall was being built an East German family tried to cross a construction site, where the wall was being made. The father, Herman, was friends with a builder, Mikhail. Mikhail promised to clear 10m along the wall. Herman shot the two guards, 'til there was 10m of room for them to run towards the wall.

As they headed towards the wall, nicely spread out, a shot rang out and the second younges child, Herr, fell to the ground. Herman and Mikhail split up, to find Herr and carry her to safety. They each searched half of the safe area, until Mikhail found Herr, and took her over the wall.

How many square metres did Mikhail search in?

A man was laying concrete next to a stone floor. When he was finished he had a 6 square meter area. He knew the width of the stone was 2 metres and the lenght was 2 metres. What area was the concrete?

Asking students to pose questions about area informs the teacher of the level of the students' understandings.

A flag that is 2m by 1·5m has an area of 3m². If you doubled its length and width, what would the area be?

If you had a 36 cm² square and you coloured in a quarter of it how much area was left of the bit of square that wasn't coloured in?

My mum and dad were going to recarpet the living room floor. It was a rectangular room that was 3m by 5m and the carpet cost $18.50 per square metre. What is the area of the room and how much would it cost?

Some problems posed on the topic of area had a practical basis.

Scaffolding Problem Writing

The girl who wrote the coloured square problem was one of several who struggled with the wording of the problem. For students who have difficulty expressing their thoughts in writing, it is important that the teacher sits with them and asks them to work out their problems orally. This is also where the teacher needs to particularly focus on students from a non-English speaking background.

In the case of the area problems, the teacher asked the students having difficulties to draw their problem first, explain in steps what they had done in their drawings, and pose a question at the end. John produced the following problem as an outcome of this process.

I ruled up a 10cm X 10cm square. I coloured a fifth of it. How big is the area that is not coloured in?

John's written problem was based on his flow chart diagrams.

Sharing Students' Problems

Students and teachers should share their problems regularly. They may be shared with the whole class or with a smaller group, or they may be made available for others to read at their leisure. Sharing their problems enhances students' communication skills as they strive to make their problems unambiguous. It also gives a purpose to the writing of problems.

The teacher's role in sharing times is to encourage and support students to use initiative in devising, explaining and refining their own problem solving strategies, including their own techniques for estimating, adding, multiplying, dividing and subtracting numbers. A regular time could be set aside each day for sharing problems.

In one Year 4 classroom, the students come into class after the recess break and immediately begin writing problems in personal problem books. As they finish, they join the teacher and their classmates on the floor to share some of the problems that have been written. Students form a circle and use MAB blocks as the basic material for supporting mental computation to work out the problems. One child has control of the MAB ones, another the tens, another the hundreds and another the thousands. Sometimes individuals use calculators or pencil and paper, and sometimes the teacher leads the children to use a large sheet of paper to do written calculations.

An alternative arrangement is for the teacher to suggest a time for discussion of particular problems so that students know they have to give them some consideration beforehand. With problems that have been written on sheets on the wall for all to see clearly, a proposed discussion time can be recorded against problems.

If, for example, 'Thursday, 10 a.m.' is written against a group of the children's problems, the children can spend time before then working alone or in a small group to solve the problems. When discussion time comes around the children can all gather together to share the work they have done.

I have used this method very successfully with upper primary classes whose daily timetable includes some 'personal study time' during which they can choose to work on problems.

Investigating

The Investigation Process

To outline the investigation process, I will describe a particular investigation: *Odd and even numbers*. This topic is a good starting point for investigative work in middle and upper primary years. It offers the potential for simple investigations and most students can offer some comments about odd and even numbers.

Beginning an investigation

When children investigate a topic they begin by sharing what they already know. In one class, the children made the following contributions when asked what they knew about odd and even numbers.

Six is even.

The numbers go odd, even, odd, even.

Even numbers have pairs, and odds have an extra.

It is a good idea to write down the students comments on a board or sheet of paper as they will form the focus of further steps. This will also demonstrate 'note making' as a way of working.

The language students use to explain ideas

It is essential to allow students to express their ideas in their own language. Too often, teachers introduce formal mathematical terminology prematurely, leading to misunderstandings and frustration.

Formal terminology should only be introduced in the context of helping students explain mathematical ideas. The right time to introduce a formal term is when the students see a need for it, or when the teacher can see it would be helpful for students to know it. For instance, a child's comment that:

… numbers can be odd or even…

can lead a teacher to challenge the child's understanding by asking a question such as:

What about numbers like one-and-a-half?

What the child means in this situation is that **whole numbers** are either odd or even, and this is an appropriate opportunity to introduce this type of terminology. In these ways, children develop their understandings and use of language, and formal terms can be introduced meaningfully.

Before this stage can be reached, students need a lot of experience in explaining their thinking and defining mathematical concepts using their own language.

Teacher: Kate, you described the difference between an odd number and an even number. You said even numbers have pairs and odds have an extra. What does everyone think of the way Kate described them? Can anyone think of other ways to describe them? Could anyone draw a picture that would show the difference?

Writing a definition

Developing a definition of a mathematical term is a key investigative task, and the focus of the teacher's questions above, is forming definitions of odd and even numbers. When students write a report of an investigation, it is often important to include a definition. Many students like to begin a report with a definition, followed by examples which are often illustrated. Some examples follow. They may not all be grammatically or mathematically correct but they are good examples of clear thinking.

An even number is a number that can be counted to by twos if you start with two. Like, 2, 4, 6, 8, 10. An odd number is the numbers in between.

An even number is one you can make into pairs with blocks and an odd number has an odd one as well as pairs. Four is even and five is odd.

Searching for patterns

Searching for patterns is a basic investigative task, and the idea of looking for patterns should be introduced very early into investigations.

Teacher:You've described some patterns such as numbers going odd, even, odd, even. What other patterns can you find? If we write a lot of numbers and find which ones are odd and which ones are even, might we find some more patterns?

The students can follow this suggestion, with the teacher moving amongst them as they work, asking what patterns they've found. At the end of the session, the students can gather again to discuss their work.

Even numbers end in zero or two or four or six or eight. Odd numbers end in one or three or five or seven or nine.

An odd plus an odd gives an even.

One is an interesting number. If you add it to an odd number you get an even number and if you add it to an even number you get an odd number.

Posing questions

It is particularly empowering for students to see their ideas valued as starting points for further work.

Teacher: It is interesting that you said an odd number plus another odd number gives an even number. What happens when you add two even numbers, or three odd numbers? What happens when you subtract an odd number from an odd number? Can you think of some other questions like this?

Often, a teacher will only need to begin a list of such questions and the students will add to the list quite spontaneously. Involving students in posing the questions is a very important aspect of successful investigative work as posing their own questions often enthuses them about seeking answers. The questions can be written on posters for display and used at another time as the basis for further investigation.

The following framework for an investigation was developed by a Year 4 class when the topic of investigating odd and even numbers had been discussed.

★ Talk about what you already know about odd and even numbers.

★ Explain what an odd number is and what an even number is.

★ Draw some pictures to help you explain what odd and even numbers are. Give some examples.

★ Write down lots of odd numbers and even numbers and look for patterns.

★ Ask some questions about odd and even numbers.

Group Work

Establishing working groups

After a general class discussion of a topic, students can work in groups of three or four on their investigations. Sometimes students like to work independently while sitting with a group and sharing their ideas, while at other times members of a group can work more closely together and a group report can be produced.

Single-sex groups are ideal at the early stage of investigative work as they allow the full participation of every student. Single-sex groups facilitate cooperative work, risk-taking and a range of involvement by all of the members.

Bringing groups together

As the students work in their small single-sex groups, the teacher can move amongst them, assisting where necessary and challenging misconceptions. Often it is useful to suggest a group discusses their work with another group who may have produced similar results, a group who may have produced contradictory results, or one who may have taken the work a step further. This gives opportunities for girls and boys to mix productively.

It is important that each investigation conclude with a class discussion time when students share what they have found. This lends further purpose to the investigation, and often sets the scene for further work. This forum also gives boys and girls a chance to work together. Having had a chance to explore their ideas in a small group, many students are more confident to express their ideas to the whole class.

Report Writing

As they work, some students ask what the teacher requires of them in terms of written work:

Whatever you think you need…

would be a suitable response at this stage. It is important that a teacher not dictate a structure for written work as this can destroy the delightful spontaneity of students' work, and limit possibilities. It is exciting for a teacher to find a range of styles of written reporting within a class. Open-ended report writing presents another avenue for students' growth as they continue to improve their reporting.

Reports can take different forms. They can be written by hand or on a computer, integrating word processing and graphics, produced as a slide show on a computer, written in a booklet or presented on a poster.

Note making

Some children make notes as they investigate, and sometimes notes are all that is needed in terms of written work, with students called on to give oral reports of their investigations while referring to their notes. This is particularly the case when the teacher wants the whole class to work together to produce a report in order to demonstrate specific report writing skills.

It is really important to involve students in occasional discussions about how they work, and one example of a discussion focus is note making. They can discuss how note making is useful for written reporting. Some students like to make notes as they work and prepare a report at the end of an investigation, others write their findings in report form as they proceed through an investigation, but try out some ideas in note form first.

While at times notes are enough of a written record of work, at other times full written reports are necessary. The teacher can discuss with students the need for a written record to be kept of their investigative work, as a useful reference for themselves for later work, a record for the teacher to show what each student has achieved, and a record for anyone, such as their parents, who would be interested in their work.

When students gather to share their findings, they can be asked to bring with them any written work they did. It is interesting to ask them to share their written work, asking why they did it the way they did. Some children will have made notes as they worked, some will have made lists of numbers with lines, arrows, circles and similar symbols to show relationships, and some will have made a full written record of what they did.

In discussing ways to write reports, it is useful for children to look at reports they have written on non-mathematical topics. For instance, how might they structure a report on frogs? Would the same structure work for a report of a mathematics investigation?

Perhaps the focus could be narrower. Have students focus on just the introduction to a report on frogs, as this usually sets the style for the whole report. Some students might begin with a definition of a frog, some might begin with a comment explaining their interest in frogs, some might begin with a question to the reader. The same approaches can be used in writing mathematics reports.

Look at the following two introductions to reports that demonstrate different approaches. The first takes a personal perspective in posing questions, while the second is strictly factual, beginning with a definition and examples.

> I wondered what I could find out about multiplying odd and even numbers. I tried small numbers first (below 10) and then did it with larger numbers to see if it still worked the same. I thought that it would but I wasn't sure.

Even numbers are made up of twos.
Like 4 is even because it is 2 and 2.
6 is even because it is 2 and 2 and 2. Odd
numbers have one extra as well as the
twos. 7 is odd. It is 2 and 2 and 2 and 1.

The approach to posing questions can differ between personal and factual.

Making diagrams

The use of diagrams should be encouraged as they help children visualise numbers, shapes, measurements, statistics and relationships. Visualising is a very important skill in mathematics. Diagrams are also a useful way of sharing ideas with others. When a student makes a verbal comment to the class, the teacher can ask them to show what they mean with a diagram or model. For instance, if a student says that even numbers are made up of twos, they could be asked to use blocks or a sketch to show what they mean. Those students who think of two as a numeral rather than a pair of objects will be particularly helped by this exercise.

Students should use concrete materials such as Unifix cubes to explore a topic like odd and even numbers, and they can be encouraged to draw pictures of the models they make with the materials, as a further record of their work and a helpful illustration of a concept for a reader.

Modelling report writing

After working on the topic: *Odd and even numbers*, the teacher can lead the class to write a report of their work. A Year 5/6 class report on odd and even numbers follows. It directly quotes the words the students used.

The first statement in the report was later challenged by the teacher:

Is it true that numbers are either odd or even? What about one-and-a-half?

The final remark in the report refers to a tables matrix that was on display in the room.

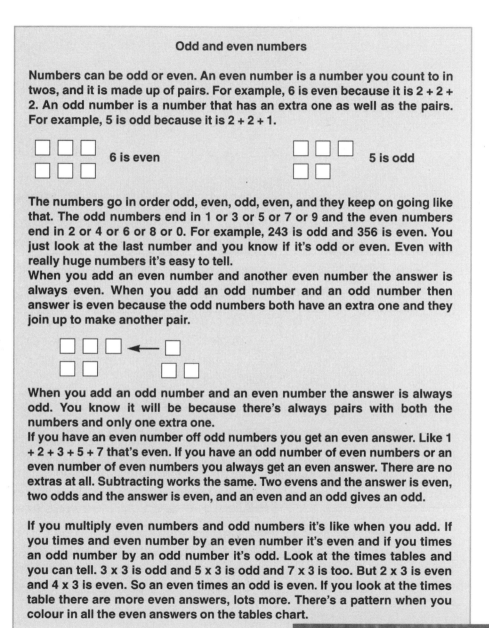

Odd and even numbers

Numbers can be odd or even. An even number is a number you count to in twos, and it is made up of pairs. For example, 6 is even because it is 2 + 2 + 2. An odd number is a number that has an extra one as well as the pairs. For example, 5 is odd because it is 2 + 2 + 1.

6 is even   5 is odd

The numbers go in order odd, even, odd, even, and they keep on going like that. The odd numbers end in 1 or 3 or 5 or 7 or 9 and the even numbers end in 2 or 4 or 6 or 8 or 0. For example, 243 is odd and 356 is even. You just look at the last number and you know if it's odd or even. Even with really huge numbers it's easy to tell.

When you add an even number and another even number the answer is always even. When you add an odd number and an odd number then answer is even because the odd numbers both have an extra one and they join up to make another pair.

When you add an odd number and an even number the answer is always odd. You know it will be because there's always pairs with both the numbers and only one extra one.

If you have an even number off odd numbers you get an even answer. Like 1 + 2 + 3 + 5 + 7 that's even. If you have an odd number of even numbers or an even number of even numbers you always get an even answer. There are no extras at all. Subtracting works the same. Two evens and the answer is even, two odds and the answer is even, and an even and an odd gives an odd.

If you multiply even numbers and odd numbers it's like when you add. If you times and even number by an even number it's even and if you times an odd number by an odd number it's odd. Look at the times tables and you can tell. 3 x 3 is odd and 5 x 3 is odd and 7 x 3 is too. But 2 x 3 is even and 4 x 3 is even. So an even times an odd is even. If you look at the times table there are more even answers, lots more. There's a pattern when you colour in all the even answers on the tables chart.

A Year 5/6 class report on odd and even numbers.

Reviewing an Investigation

When an investigation has been completed, the class can review what they have learned about the topic and about the investigative process. Such a review can be done through discussion, firstly in working groups and later in a whole class gathering.

At this stage the teacher can challenge the children to apply their new understandings and knowledge to tasks such as the following related to odd and even numbers.

★ How can you use a calculator to generate the sequence of odd numbers?

★ How can you work out what is the 11th even number?

★ What is the largest even number you can show on your calculator?

★ What number comes next in this sequence: 50, 49, 46, 41, 34?

★ What number comes next in this sequence: 2, 6, 12, 20, 30?

★ I'm thinking of an even number between 10 and 20. If you halve the number you get another even number and if you halve that number you get an even number again. What is the number I'm thinking of?

★ Find three consecutive even numbers that add to 30.

★ Find two odd numbers whose sum is 20 and whose difference is 6.

These tasks build on what children know about odd and even numbers and challenge them to find ways to work out answers. They also extend children's use of mathematical language. For example, the two tasks seeking the next number in a sequence can lead to the introduction of the terms: **consecutive odd numbers** and **consecutive even numbers**. Children can be encouraged to set similar tasks for their classmates.

Addition

Single-digit Addition Strategies

The first concept to be understood by students when embarking on investigating computation strategies is the concept of a **strategy**. The following account is a discussion of the term strategy in a Year 4/5 class.

Teacher: Can anyone tell us what they think is meant by the word strategy?

It's like in a football match. A team has a strategy. It's a plan of how they're going to play the game.

It's a way to solve a maths problem.

Any kind of problem.

It's a way to do something.

T: *You've got a pretty good idea of what strategy means. I'm going to say a number, then choose someone to add ten to that number, then after that another person to add ten to that number and so on. We'll keep adding ten. Eight. Kate, can you add ten to eight?*

Eighteen

T: *Matt?*

Twenty-eight

T: *Laurie?*

Thirty-eight

Several students were called upon to add ten.

Teacher: Now, who can explain the strategy they used to add ten?

Well you imagine the number is made of tens and ones. You just add a ten so there's still the same number of ones and there's one more ten so if you started with forty-eight you go up one more ten to fifty-eight.

T: Great. Now let's see what happens when we add nine to a number. I'll start with sixteen. Rowan, can you start us off by adding the first nine?

Several students took turns to add nine.

Teacher: Who can explain the strategy they used to add nine?

I added ten then took one off.

I went back one then I added ten.

The teacher then set the students the task of investigating patterns produced by repeatedly adding nine. She sat with four students who did not seem confident about using the word strategy.

Teacher: Let's look at what the word strategy means. First I'll give you a problem to work out.

★ If you had 4 apples and 3 bananas, how many pieces of fruit would you have?

The students counted on their fingers and gave the correct answer.

Teacher: Now let's see how you worked out the answer. What strategy did you use?

Ruqayah looked puzzled at first, then looked down at her hand.

Hand?

Teacher: How did you use your hand?

I counted on my fingers.

T: Right. Counting on your fingers is the strategy you used. What strategy did you others use?

They all said they had counted on their fingers.

Teacher: If I gave you some blocks to work out the answer, what strategy would you use?

I'd count the blocks.

T: *OK. Now all of you have a go at working out this problem.*

★ **If you each have 6 Unifix cubes and you put them together how many would there be?**

They counted out six Unifix cubes each, combined them and counted them.

Teacher: What strategy did you use to find the answer this time?

We put the Unifix cubes together and counted them.

T: *Good. Now I would like the four of you to talk about what the word strategy means. I'm going to see what the others are doing at their tables while you do that. I'll come back in a few minutes to see what you have done. Kehau, please check that all four of you have a turn at speaking.*

Once students are familiar with the concept of a strategy, they can investigate many different strategies and discuss them from time to time to continually reinforce them.

★ **How do you add 2?**

★ **What strategy do you use to add 3 to another number?**

★ **If you are adding 8 and 4, how do you do it?**

★ **If you have a lot of numbers to add, like 2 + 3 + 7 + 6 + 8, how might you do it?**

A discussion of strategies for adding eight produced the following comments from some Year 4/5 students.

With the eight I took part of it to make up a ten and then I added the rest. If I was adding eight to fourteen I would take six out of the eight to make the fourteen up to twenty then that would leave two more so it's twenty-two.

I did the same. I added some of the eight to reach a number with zero on the end, then I added the rest of the eight to that number to come up with the answer.

The strategy I used for adding eight was I added ten to the number then I minused two from the answer because ten minus two is eight and it makes it simpler to do it that way.

I added one to the tens column and took two away from the ones column. But if I added eight to a number ending in zero, one or two, I couldn't do it that way but they're easy anyway.

The addition of five makes an interesting investigation. One Year 4 class was set the following investigation:

★ Investigate the patterns that are produced when you add 5 to any number.

Here are some of the comments the children made.

When you add five to a number ending in one you always get a number ending in six.

When you add five to a number ending in two you always get a number ending in seven.

When you add five to a number ending in three you always get a number ending in eight.

It's really interesting because you add five to a number with a four on the end and you get a number with a nine on the end then you add five to the answer and you get a four on the end. I'll show you what I mean. 14 + 5 = 19 then 19 + 5 = 24. I think it's because five is half of ten and when you add five twice it's like you're adding ten.

Addition Chains

Addition chains were invented by a group of Year 4 students who defined them as follows:

An addition chain begins with one and keeps on adding the same number until it finishes with a number ending in one (like eleven or twenty-one).

Adding one

$1 \longrightarrow 2 \longrightarrow 3 \longrightarrow 4 \longrightarrow 5 \longrightarrow 6 \longrightarrow 7 \longrightarrow 8 \longrightarrow 9 \longrightarrow 10 \longrightarrow 11$

(Ten steps to get from 1 to 11.)

Adding two

$1 \longrightarrow 3 \longrightarrow 5 \longrightarrow 7 \longrightarrow 9 \longrightarrow 11$ (Five steps)

Adding three

$1 \longrightarrow 4 \longrightarrow 7 \longrightarrow 10 \longrightarrow 13 \longrightarrow 16 \longrightarrow 19 \longrightarrow 22 \longrightarrow 25 \longrightarrow 28 \longrightarrow 31$

(Ten steps)

Adding four

$1 \longrightarrow 5 \longrightarrow 9 \longrightarrow 13 \longrightarrow 17 \longrightarrow 21$ (Five steps)

Adding five

$1 \longrightarrow 6 \longrightarrow 11$ (Two steps)

Adding six

$1 \longrightarrow 7 \longrightarrow 13 \longrightarrow 19 \longrightarrow 25 \longrightarrow 31$ (Five steps)

Adding seven

$1 \longrightarrow 8 \longrightarrow 15 \longrightarrow 22 \longrightarrow 29 \longrightarrow 36 \longrightarrow 43 \longrightarrow 50 \longrightarrow 57 \longrightarrow 64 \longrightarrow 71$

(Ten steps)

Adding eight

$1 \longrightarrow 9 \longrightarrow 17 \longrightarrow 25 \longrightarrow 33 \longrightarrow 41$ (Five steps)

Adding nine

$1 \longrightarrow 10 \longrightarrow 19 \longrightarrow 28 \longrightarrow 37 \longrightarrow 46 \longrightarrow 55 \longrightarrow 64 \longrightarrow 73 \longrightarrow 82 \longrightarrow 91$

(Ten steps)

The children found that it takes five steps for all even numbers and ten steps for all odd numbers except five. The children also noted that the final number in each of the chains where an odd number was added (except five) has the tens digit matching this number. For example, when seven is added, the final number in the chain is seventy-one. When an even number is added the tens digit in this final number is half the number being added. For example, when four is added, the final number in the chain is twenty-one.

A discussion of why the chain generated by the addition of five is different can be linked to looking at the addition of five described earlier. The children can note the fact that five is half of ten makes it behave in certain interesting ways.

Adding Two-digit Numbers

Mental addition

To introduce this topic in an appropriate context, the teacher collects several problems written by the students that involve adding two-digit numbers. Students are set the task of investigating ways to work out the answers to such problems, preferably mentally.

They should begin by estimating the answer to a calculation. The act of estimating will focus the children's attention on the numbers, on making sense of the problem and its solution, and on mental computation.

Here is a problem written by a Year 4 student.

★ If I had $36 in the bank and I got $25 for my birthday, how much money would I have then?

The teacher suggested the children estimate the answer, and for many this quickly led to the correct answer.

Fifty something dollars.

50… no, 60… $61!

When one Year 4 class shared their methods for mentally adding two-digit numbers, the following ones were revealed. Most of the children worked from left to right.

We started with the tens then we added the ones.

Sometimes it's easy. You can just see how many tens there are and how many ones there are, but sometimes there's a lot of ones and that's harder.

You can write down how many tens there are so you don't get in a muddle when you're adding the ones.

I started with the tens too. If there's more than nine ones you have to change some into tens. But that's easy. You just have to remember how many tens you've already got.

Teacher: How would you add sixty-three and twenty-one and seventy-nine?

Well there's six, eight, fifteen tens, that's 150. Then there's thirteen ones so that's another ten, 160. 163.

Look! twenty-one and seventy-nine is 100. So it's 163.

T: So sometimes you can find a shortcut.

When working mentally, many students need the support of a visual or concrete model of the numbers they are working with. Materials such as MAB blocks should always be on hand for this purpose. Students can also be helped to find ways to draw models of numbers, using symbols to represent ones, tens, hundreds etc. Dots, circles or crosses can be ones, long lines can be tens and squares can be hundreds, as these symbols all look similar to the MAB representations of these numbers.

Written addition

Children work in groups to devise written strategies for adding pairs or lists of two-digit numbers. Children are given one computation to work on (e.g. 67 + 83 + 38), then after they have checked their answer on a calculator, reworked it if incorrect, and discussed their strategy with the teacher, they can be given another. In this way, groups of children are introduced to increasingly complex examples.

Once they have devised a successful written strategy, they explain it in writing, step by step. Later, each group exchange their written instructions with those of another group and test the method devised by the other group, comparing the methods generated.

The teacher models a standard written algorithm and asks students to explain why it works, or the students can be led to develop the standard algorithm themselves. The following is an account of a lesson with a group of six Year 4 children who had encountered a standard addition algorithm in their previous year in school and been unsuccessful in understanding and using it. The teacher started with a problem involving money because she knew most of the children were fairly confident handling money, particularly when buying chocolate bars and similar treats.

Teacher: Let's sit together and have a look at doing some addition.

I'm no good at adding.

T: Don't bring your pencils and paper, we're going to do it in our heads.

That's too hard. I can't do it.

T: Well, let's give it a go. Now let's say you were shopping and bought two chocolate bars for forty cents each. How much would that cost you?

Eighty cents. But that's easy.

T: Why is that easy?

Because you just know forty and forty is eighty.

T: What if they were forty-three cents each?

Eighty-six cents.

T: You did that quickly. How did you work it out?

Well, that's forty and forty, eighty, and two threes, eighty-six.

T: What if the chocolate bars were different prices. Let's see, one of them is forty-six cents and the other is forty-three cents.

That's eighty. Eighty-something cents. What did they cost?

T: I'll write the prices down so you remember them.

Eighty-nine cents.

T: How did you work that out?

I said forty and forty is eighty and then I added six and three. This is easy.

I help my dad in his hire shop and I do the money sometimes. Money's easy.

T: Try this one. How much would you spend if the chocolate bars were forty-eight cents and forty-three cents? (She writes the prices down.)

Easy! Eighty. Huh? No, it's more than eighty-something.

Eighty... no, no... ninety... ninety-one cents!

T: Great! Why did you think it was eighty-something then change your minds?

Because eight cents and three cents, that's more than ten cents so you have to go past the eighty cents up to ninety.

And you take two of the cents from the three cents to make up to ninety cents and then there's just one more cent so it's got to be ninety-one cents.

T: *Did you find it helpful when I wrote the prices down?*

Yes, because it's hard to remember them sometimes.

T: *Well, when you do written addition, the numbers are written down to help you remember them. Then you just need to work them out in your head like you've been doing. I'll give you some to try together and I'll go and check on what everyone else is doing.*

A later lesson with the group focused on the standard written algorithm.

Teacher: You're all doing so well with addition now. I think today we can look at the way you were shown how to do written addition last year and see if it makes sense. Who can start us off with a problem where we have to add some two-digit numbers?

I've got thirty-one different stamps from Australia and twelve from England. How many is that?

Forty-three.

T: *OK. Let's see how that would look if we wrote it. Who could do that for us?*

Joseph writes
$$\begin{array}{r} 31 \\ +12 \\ \hline 43 \end{array}$$

Teacher: Right, let's try a harder one. What if Myfanwy had thirty-six Australian stamps and seventeen English stamps? How many would that be?

(She writes the numbers as she says them.)
$$\begin{array}{r} 36 \\ +17 \\ \hline \end{array}$$

Teacher: When you've been adding these numbers in your heads you've started with the tens. What will happen if you start from the other side and do the ones first?

You mean six plus seven?

T: Yes, will that be useful?

Six plus seven is thirteen. Oh, now you can put the ten from the thirteen with the thirty and the ten.

That's fifty. So it's fifty-three.

T: *That's right, Craig. Can you show the others how you did that?*

Craig demonstrated his method and the others liked it. They tried some more examples as a group, without the teacher's help. The teacher stayed with the group, observing them and giving positive feedback. At this stage the children were not recording the number in the ones column until they had completed their calculation. A later lesson dealt with this.

The next lesson began with a review of Craig's method and continued as follows.

Teacher: When people do the addition Craig's way, they usually write the answer starting from the right hand end. For instance, if the answer is forty-five, they write the five first. Why do you think they do that?

She writes

$$\begin{array}{r} 27 \\ + \ 18 \\ \hline 45 \end{array}$$

Well they work out the ones first… but if there's fifteen ones you can't put fifteen down because that doesn't make sense.

I don't know.

T: *If you were working out twenty-seven plus eighteen using Craig's way, what is the first part of the answer that you know, the five or the forty?*

The first bit we do is the seven plus eight and that's fifteen.

… The five, I think.

T: *Let's add sixty-eight and twenty-four, and see what part of the answer you know first.*

Eight plus four is… twelve. You know the two first. That's got to be on the end of the answer.

T: *Aimee, that's great. Can you explain that to the rest of the group, please? Then you can all try some more to see if it works.*

Spreadsheet addition

Children can construct addition tables using computer spreadsheets. The following table is an example created by a group of 10 and 11 year olds. Using a formula, they added zero across row one, one across row two, two across row three, etc. Then they totalled each row and column.

1	1	1	1	1	1	1	1	1	1	11
2	3	4	5	6	7	8	9	10	11	66
3	5	7	9	11	13	15	17	19	21	121
4	7	10	13	16	19	22	25	28	31	176
5	9	13	17	21	25	29	33	37	41	231
6	11	16	21	26	31	36	41	46	51	286
7	13	19	25	31	37	43	49	55	61	341
8	15	22	29	36	43	50	57	64	71	396
9	17	25	33	41	49	57	65	73	81	451
10	19	28	37	46	55	64	73	82	91	506
11	21	31	41	51	61	71	81	91	101	561
66	121	176	231	286	341	396	451	506	561	3146

Spreadsheet addition table generated on a computer.

The children discovered many patterns in the table and used mental computation to attempt to explain the patterns. For example, they worked out that the row and column totals increased by fifty-five each time.

Addition Practice through Investigations

All the practice children need at working algorithms can be provided by investigations. There are many possible investigation topics that give children purposeful addition practice.

★ What happens when you add numbers ending in 9 to numbers ending in 3 (e.g. 29 + 33)?

★ What happens when you add 14 to numbers ending in 8 (e.g. 8 + 14, 18 + 14, 28 + 14)?

★ Investigate what happens when you add two-digit palindromes such as 66 + 77 or 77 + 99 + 88.

★ If you add any consecutive numbers, which answers will you never get? (The answer is: the numbers in the binary sequence.)

★ Investigate what happens when you add 3 consecutive numbers… 3 consecutive even numbers… 3 consecutive odd numbers… 5 consecutive odd numbers.

Here is an account by a group of girls who investigated adding consecutive even numbers. The original question was:

★ What happens when you add 3 consecutive even numbers?

Adding consecutive even numbers

We tried adding 3 consecutive even numbers. Here are some consecutive even numbers in order and what they add up to.

2+4+6=12
4+6+8=18
6+8+10=24
8+10+12=30
10+12+14=36
12+14+16=42
14+16+18=48
16+18+20=54
18+20+22=60

We found out that the answers are the ×6 table but 6 is missing. You can get 6 if you go 0+2+4=6 but we don't know if 0 is an even number.

Next we tried 4 consecutive even numbers.

0+2+4+6=12
2+4+6+8=20
4+6+8+10=28
6+8+10+12=36
8+10+12+14=44

10+12+14+16=52

The answers are every second number in the ×4 table but 4 is missing so we tried how to get 4. We did -2+0+2+4=4 and you can see it worked

Group work: adding even consecutive numbers.

The group went on to add five then six consecutive even numbers and later said to the teacher:

We didn't know much about minus numbers before but they're really good and we can understand them. They just fitted the pattern and we figured out how to add them.

When the group shared their work with the class, the teacher suggested the class work together to add seven consecutive even numbers, then nine, without looking at the negative numbers. This gave the class an opportunity to not only search for patterns but to revisit the addition strategy of **looking for tens**. For example, when adding $0 + 2 + 4 + 6 + 8 + 10 + 12$, the children paired two and eight and four and six to make the addition simpler.

Adding Larger Numbers

As with the addition of two-digit numbers, the problems children write are used to introduce the addition of larger numbers. Emma, in Year 4, wrote the following problem.

★ Me and Renee are collecting Pen Pal books. We have 4 so far. *Sam the Sham* has 117 pages, *No Creeps Need Apply* has 134 pages, *Amy's Song* has 135 pages and *P.S. Forget It* has 114 pages. How many pages have we got so far?

Emma's problem was presented to the class to solve in pairs. Later, the children shared their answers and the strategies they used.

We got the hundreds first. There were four hundreds. Then we did the tens and that was eighty. Then there were twenty ones which are really two more tens. That was tricky because then we had ten tens so that meant we had five hundreds. The answer's 500.

Many of the other children were enthusiastic about the book series problem and they began posing similar ones, finding the number of pages in sets of encyclopedias and other series of books. The teacher posed the following problem.

★ I collect series of books, too. One of the series has books with this many pages: 317, 319, 285, 271, 380, 284. How can you use written addition to work out how many pages are in this series of books?

Investigation topics also give purposeful practice in adding larger numbers.

★ What happens when you add numbers ending in 77 to numbers ending in 33 (e.g. 477 + 833)? From your answer, can you predict what will happen when you add numbers ending in 67 to numbers ending in 33?

★ Investigate adding numbers formed by three consecutive digits to their reverse (e.g. 123 + 321, 234 + 432, 345 + 543, 456 + 654).

★ Investigate what happens when you begin with any three-digit number, reverse it and add the reversed number to the original number, repeating the process until a palindrome is reached.

When one group of students worked on the task:

★ What happens when you add a number ending in 4 to a number ending in 7?

they produced the following algorithm.

```
  474747
+ 747474
 1222221
```

They liked the pattern of the answer and diverged from the set task to produce a series of algorithms with similar answers, such as: 383838 + 838383 and 292929 + 929292. Later, they produced other answers with algorithms such as 484848 + 848484. This task provided lots of purposeful addition practice for the class as everyone became enthusiastic about the patterns.

Adding Decimals

When adding decimals, it is very important that students estimate the answer at the outset as this helps them place the decimal point correctly in the answer. For example, if a child estimates the sum of 6.25 and 3.5 to be:

Nine point something…

they are likely to realise an answer such as 6.6 (which they could get if they set out the algorithm inappropriately) is wrong.

Through investigations, students are assisted to make links between the addition of decimals and the addition of whole numbers. Calculators are important tools for these investigations, supporting children as they work towards devising strategies for adding decimals.

A first investigation might be:

★ Use mental addition and a calculator to investigate the
   following calculations:

65 + 32	34 + 25	70 + 25	$125 + $350
6.5 + 3.2	3.4 + 2.5	7.0 + 2.5	$1.25 + $3.50

Other investigations could include the following.

★ Work out the answer to the following without using a
   calculator: 2.5 + 6.75 + 10.25. Now check your answer with a
   calculator. Now do the same with: 3.4 + 2.6 + 6.45. What is a
   good strategy for working out this type of calculation on
   paper?

★ Investigate using a calculator to add amounts of money. Try
   $1.25 + $1.35 and $1.50 + $2.40, as well as your own examples.
   What do you notice?

★ Work with a partner on this investigation. If one of you stands
   on the other one's shoulders, how high can you reach? If your
   positions are reversed, can you reach the same height? (Find
   a strategy to work out the answer without actually standing
   on each other's shoulders as this could be dangerous.)

This investigation involves the children adding measurements using metres
and centimetres.

Triangular Numbers

The sequence of triangular numbers, which is generated by adding
consecutive numbers from one, is an interesting topic of study and provides
practice in addition. It is introduced by the teacher writing the first few
numbers in the sequence (without naming the sequence) and asking
students to explore how the sequence might continue. The students are set
the task of making models of the numbers and working out a name for the
sequence. Some students will suggest the term **staircase numbers** and their
models will resemble staircases. Other students will produce the following
diagrams of their models and the term **triangular numbers** can be related
to their models.

```
  X              X                    X                          X
        X   X              X   X                      X   X
                      X   X   X                   X   X   X
                                              X   X   X   X
```

These number models are called triangular numbers due to their triangular shape.

Students observe that the sequence is arrived at by adding another row to the preceding model, or that the sequence is a result of adding consecutive numbers from one. They may also note that the sequence begins with two odd numbers, then proceeds with two even numbers, then two odd numbers, and so on; they can be challenged to explain why this occurs.

A challenging task is to find a method for producing a particular triangular number, such as the fifth triangular number or the sixteenth triangular number. A group of Year 6 students worked out an excellent method after a good deal of work, listing many triangular numbers and searching for relationships. As the group worked on the task, they produced the following sequence of ideas. To explain their work, they invented the term **starting number**. The starting number of the third triangular number is three and the starting number of the sixth triangular number is six and so on. The students first noticed the following pattern for every odd starting number.

Starting number	Multiplied by	Gives the triangular number
1	1	1
3	2	6
5	3	15
7	4	28
9	5	45
11	6	66

The students realised they had to work out a way to know what to multiply a starting number by. For instance, if they wanted to know the thirty-first triangular number, they needed to know what to multiply it by. They looked carefully at the numbers in their table and saw that if they added one to the starting number and halved it they would know what number to multiply by. So thirty-one would be multiplied by sixteen, which is half of thirty-two.

Then even starting numbers were reviewed.

Starting number	Triangular number
2	3
4	10
6	21
8	36
10	55

At first the students could not find a relationship between the starting number and its triangular number. The teacher asked the students if they could apply the same method as they did to the odd starting numbers, and they found that it worked. Some students produced the following table to explain an alternative method.

starting number	Add one to the starting number	halve the starting number	Multiply them
1.	1+1=2	½ of 1 = ½	2 × ½ = 1
2.	2+1=3	½ of 2 = 1	3 × 1 = 3
3.	3+1=4	½ of 3 = 1½	4 × 1½ = 6
4.	4+1=5	½ of 4 = 2	5 × 2 = 10
5.	5+1=6	½ of 5 = 2½	6 × 2½ = 15
6.	6+1=7	½ of 6 = 3	7 × 3 = 21

Triangular numbers occur in the solutions to some problems; some of these follow.

Handshakes problem
There were 3 people at a meeting. If they all shook hands with each other, how many handshakes would there be? What if a fourth person came? A fifth? A sixth?

Investigating the number of sides and diagonals in regular polygons also produces the sequence of triangular numbers. If students make diagrams to model the handshakes problem above, their diagrams may be the regular polygons.

Triangles within triangles problem
How many triangles can be found in the following diagram? If students work systematically, counting the triangles by size and orientation ($\triangle$ or $\triangledown$), they will encounter triangular numbers.

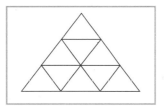

Making numbers problem
How many numbers can be made from the following digits? 001 (100 is the only number), 0011 (three possibilities: 1100, 1010, 1001), 00111 (six possibilities: 11100, 11010, 11001, 10101, 10011, 10110) etc.

Paths problem
In the following diagrams, look for the shortest paths possible along the lines to get from the bottom left hand corner to the top right hand corner.

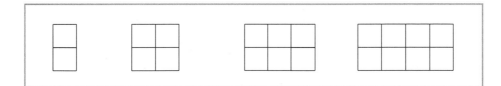

There are three possible paths in the first diagram, six in the second, ten in the third and fifteen in the fourth.

Fibonacci Numbers

The following lesson introduces the Fibonacci sequence; the sequence of numbers generated by adding the last two numbers in the sequence.

Teacher: I'm going to start writing a sequence of numbers on the whiteboard. What do you think comes next?

She writes one, two, three and the students all expect the next number to be four.

Teacher: No, it's not four.

It can't be anything else.

It could be six.

T: Why do you think it could be six?

Because you start with one then you double it, then you add one, then you double that.

T: Good thinking, Tom. But it's not six this time.

There are no more suggestions other than some guesses. The teacher adds five to the sequence.

Huh? That doesn't make sense.

The teacher adds an eight.

You could be adding the last two numbers because three plus five is eight.

Thirteen is added to the sequence.

Yes, you're adding the last two numbers.

T: You're right. Let's look at the beginning of the sequence. Is there something wrong there?

The two. If you put another one at the beginning you could put two after that.

So the sequence reads 1… 1… 2… 3… 5… 8… 13… 21 and so on. The following set of problems provides further opportunity to explore the Fibonacci sequence.

★ Imagine a set of stairs with 3 steps and a child who likes to play on the stairs. The child can climb the stairs one at a time, two at a time or a combination of both. How many different ways can the child climb the stairs from bottom to top?

★ What if there are 4 steps? 5? 6? 7?

Pascal's Triangle

At the end of a school year, students enjoy this activity based on Pascal's Triangle. It requires a very large copy of the following diagram, with each square measuring about eight by eight centimetres.

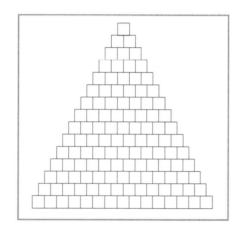

The teacher then writes one in the top square, in the squares on the ends of each row, and begins recording numbers in the other squares by adding the numbers in the two squares in the row above that touch that square. For instance, the first five rows will look like this.

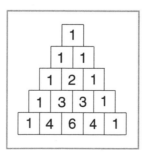

The students are asked to think about how the teacher is working out the numbers to record in the squares, and once they have done so they can help with the task. Once a few rows have been completed, students work in groups to make their own smaller versions of Pascal's Triangle. The teacher leads them to suggest how they might check their computations are correct.

We can check with each other. If we get the same answers then we're probably right.

There are probably patterns and if a number doesn't fit the pattern then it's wrong.

There is a pattern! It's like a palindrome. It is a palindrome.

It's not really a palindrome because when you've got the row with the tens it would only be a palindrome if one of the tens was written back to front.

Teacher: Good point, Patricia. But there is a way to describe the pattern you're noticing.

It's symmetrical.

There are many interesting patterns in Pascal's Triangle. Students will be able to find in the diagonals sequences such as the sequence of triangular numbers and the sequence of tetrahedral numbers.

Some students can work with the teacher on filling the squares on the large triangle and, when it is completed, all the students gather together for the next step. The teacher begins by painting with pink paint the squares marked with a one, without explaining which squares are being painted.

You're painting the ones pink, then you'll use a different colour for the twos and so on.

Then the teacher can paint the other odd numbers pink as well.

You're painting the odd numbers pink.

The teacher explains that it is possible to create patterns in Pascal's Triangle by colouring other types of numbers such as the multiples of a number. While the group which worked with the teacher on the large triangle can continue painting the odd numbered squares pink, then paint the even numbered squares a paler pink, the other groups can return to their own triangles and colour all the numbers that are a multiple of a certain number. Each group could select a different set of multiples.

The painted Pascal's Triangle, when it dries, is turned upside down and, adorned with a white beard and red hat, looks strikingly like Santa Claus.

Multiplication

Multiplication is introduced through the relevant problems children have written and through an investigation of sequences of multiples generated by repeated addition. If children have studied triangular numbers and Fibonacci numbers, they will be familiar with the concept of a number sequence.

Investigating Sequences of Multiples

Sequences of multiples are a rich source of patterns for investigation. These investigations build an understanding of number relationships, an enthusiasm for number patterns and confidence in working with numbers.

Multiples of nine

An interesting starting point is the sequence of multiples of nine as there are many patterns which children can find. If the class has discussed strategies for adding nine, this gives them a chance to practise the strategy.

To introduce an investigation of the multiples of nine, and generate children's own natural language, a teacher can begin to list multiples of nine in order, without any comment. As the students watch, many will offer suggestions quite spontaneously about the numbers.

You're counting in nines.

You're adding nine each time.

There's a pattern.

They're in the nine times table.

To introduce the idea that these numbers are named to reflect their relationship, the teacher can ask:

What could we call these numbers?

Some responses might be:

Nine numbers

Nine times table numbers

Times by nine numbers

Once students have explored various possibilities it is appropriate to introduce the term **multiples of nine**.

The teacher then asks the students how they could go about investigating the multiples of nine. They may suggest listing multiples of nine and looking for patterns. At this stage, their investigations begin. One way to generate a sequence of multiples is to use mental calculation, another is to use the constant function on a calculator.

How to do the multiples of 28 on a calculator!
Print in 28 then print in + then print in = for example say you wanted to do 8x28 you could print in 8x28= then you would get the answer or you could print in 28+==== = = = = . If you print in = 8 times you will get the answer as well. 224!

Multiples of 28→308

28
56
84
112
140
168
196
224
252
280
308

Matthew's report of the multiples of twenty-eight.

I like to establish the pattern of working out mentally the first ten or so numbers in a sequence, checking them with a calculator, then continuing the sequence either mentally or with the calculator. Many children choose to use mostly mental calculation as they are proud of being able to do so, and they find it relatively easy once they become familiar with the patterns in a sequence. There are other children who turn fairly quickly to calculators. I sometimes sit with these children and support them to do more mental calculation.

As children investigate the multiples of nine they should record what they do.

Nines

I am counting in nines.

9, 18, 27, 36, 45, 54, 63, 72, 81, 90, 108, 117, 126, 135, 144, 153, 162, 171, 180, 189, 198, 207, 216

I am going to make a list.

9	99	189
18	108	198
27	117	207
36	126	216
45	135	225
54	144	234
63	153	243
72	162	252
81	171	261
90	180	270

I found lots of patterns like the first numbers go up 1, 2, 3, 4, 5, 6, 7, 8, 9 then they go 10, 11, 12, 13, and keep going like that. Then the last numbers go down 9, 8, 7, 6, 5, 4, 3, 2, 1, 0 and they start at 9 again and go down again. If you look at the numbers going across the first row ends in 9 and the next ends in 8 and it keeps going down till you get to zero on the end. Sometimes numbers next to each other turn around. I wrote 45 and then I turned it around to get 54. I wrote 234 and turned it around to get 243

It didn't happen in the second row.

The beginning of a report written by a group of four Year 6 girls is featured next. They had made notes as they worked and wrote the report up after concluding their investigation and explaining their discoveries to their teacher. The extensive discussions they were involved in together, and with their teacher, helped them write their ideas in quite a sophisticated way.

The multiples of nine

There are some interesting patterns in the sequence of multiples of nine. Here are the first ten numbers in the sequence.

9
18
27
36
45
54
63
72
81
90

The arrows indicate one pattern
Note how the digits are reversed.

What about the next ten numbers in the sequence?

99
108
117
126
135
144
153
162
171
180

A similar pattern occurs. We wondered if this would keep on happening.

189
198
207
216
225
234
243
252
261
270
279
288
297
306

Yes! The pattern does continue
We also noticed another pattern:

108 (9 × 12)
207 (9 × 23)
306 (9 × 34)

We thought that 9×45 would be 405 following this pattern so we tried it out and we were correct.
So the pattern will continue like this:

504 (9 × 56)
603 (9 × 67)
702 (9 × 78)
801 (9 × 89)

In contrast to the report earlier, the patterns of multiples of nine can be displayed in various ways.

Reducing numbers

Very often, a few students in a class will notice that the digits of the first ten multiples, and some later multiples, add to nine. This is the technique of reducing numbers, a very useful technique for exploring patterns in number sequences.

Rather than demonstrating the process of reduction, the teacher leads children to develop the technique for themselves.

Teacher: Ismail, you said that the one and the eight in eighteen add to nine and you said the same thing happens with some of the other multiples of nine. Can you show us which ones by making a list on the whiteboard?

As Ismail does so, other students who are watching him offer other possibilities, thus sharing in the discovery.

Teacher: Who can tell me one multiple of nine that doesn't fit the pattern?

Ninety-nine.

T: Why doesn't that fit?

It can't because nine and another nine is eighteen.

T: Let's write it down... ninety-nine... it becomes eighteen. Could we do anything with the eighteen?

Well it can change to nine if you add the one and the eight. It sort of fits the pattern then.

T: How about trying other multiples of nine that don't seem to fit the pattern? Go and work in your groups to investigate this.

Multiples of four

As a contrast to the sequence of multiples of nine, it is interesting to explore the multiples of four. The investigation is introduced by the following example.

Teacher: What is special about these numbers: 4, 8, 12, 16, 20, 24, 28, 32?

They're all even.

You're counting in fours.

The next one's thirty-six then forty then forty-four.

Are they multiples of four?

T: *Yes, they are. If you investigated the multiples of four do you think you could find some interesting patterns?*

They'll all be even.

T: *Do you all agree with Matthew that all the multiples of four will be even?*

We could write them down and find out.

T: *OK, good idea. Let's investigate the multiples of four to see what we can find.*

The children will find that the multiples of four are all even, the pattern of final digits is: 4, 8, 2, 6, 0 and if they reduce the multiples they will find the sequence of reduced numbers is: 4, 8, 3, 7, 2, 6, 1, 5, 9 (repeatedly).

As students work, the teacher poses additional questions that expand the students' focus.

Teacher: If you wrote down lots of multiples of four, say the first 100, would you find more patterns than if you just wrote down ten or twenty multiples of four?

This question will lead most students to compile long lists, arranged as follows.

4	104	204	304
8	108	208	308
12	112	212	312
16	116	216	316
20	120	220	320
24	124	224	324
28	128	228	328
32	132	232	332
36	136	236	336
40	140	240	340
44	144	244	344
48	148	248	348
52	152	252	352
56	156	256	356
60	160	260	360
64	164	264	364
68	168	268	368
72	172	272	372
76	176	276	376
80	180	280	380
84	184	284	384
88	188	288	388
92	192	292	392
96	196	296	396
100	200	300	400

It is a good idea to make a large copy of this list for long-term display on the classroom wall as it will be useful for later work on the four times table, multiples of eight and twelve, square numbers, divisibility and lowest common multiples.

The teacher can challenge students to offer explanations of what they observe in the list of multiples.

Teacher: Look at the three-digit multiples of four. Is there anything interesting about the final two digits in all of these?

Yes, they're exactly the same as the first column.

They're multiples of four.

T: Why does this happen?

Because 100 is a multiple of four and the rest follow on. Then 200 is a multiple of four and the rest of those follow on.

To challenge children's understanding of the concept of multiples, one teacher set the following task.

Teacher: How would you continue the sequence of numbers that begins: 1, 5, 9, 13, 17...?

21, 25...

T: Right. How did you know that?

You were adding four all the time.

T: Do you mean I was listing the multiples of four?

No. They're not the same numbers.

T: But I added four each time. Isn't that what we did when we found the multiples of four?

But this time you didn't start with four, you started with one.

T: Let's write down the numbers in this sequence. Who'd like to write them on the whiteboard?

Look, they're all odd.

The last number in each one makes a pattern.

T: Oh yes, look at the pattern of the final digits: 1, 5, 9, 3, 7... Why do you think they're all odd?

Because we started with an odd number and we kept adding an even number.

Multiples of five and twenty-five

Links are often made between work with numbers and work on measurement and space. To introduce a sequence of multiples, students can investigate area, which is linked closely with multiplication. For instance, investigating the area of rectangles that measure 1 cm × 5 cm, 2 cm × 5 cm, 3 cm × 5 cm, 4 cm × 5 cm etc., will introduce the sequence of multiples of five.

After exploring the multiples of five, students can investigate the sequence of multiples of twenty-five. They will note that the multiples of five end in either a five or a zero, and they will now note the same for the multiples of twenty-five. The teacher can ask students why this is, and they may be able to explain that any multiple of twenty-five is also a multiple of five. The sequences are compared to explain this relationship in more detail. As one student put it:

Every fifth multiple of five is a multiple of twenty-five and that's because five times five is twenty-five. If you did the multiples of fifteen you'd have every third multiple of five the same as the multiples of fifteen.

To link again to measurement, students in one class explored the contents of their cupboards at home to find products that are measured in multiples of twenty-five (e.g. 450 g cans of fruit, 850 mL bottles of drink).

Zero as a multiple

Searching for patterns leads children to understand that zero is a multiple of any number. The following two pieces of work show the two stages in the process of understanding this concept

In both of these pieces of work Clare is interested in the pattern produced by the tens digits of the numbers in sequences of multiples. In the first example, she does not realise that her problem could be solved if she were to include zero as a multiple of twelve (i.e. 0×12). In the second example she does include zero as a multiple of twenty-four.

Twelves

Definition: A multiple of 12 is a number in the 12 times table and can be divided equally by 12. Eg. 24 ÷ 12 = 2

The multiples of 12:

12	60	108	156	204
24	72	120	168	216
36	84	132	180	228
48	96	144	192	240

Patterns:

In the ones column it counts up to 8 by twos then goes 0 and starts again. Another pattern is that if you look in the tens column you see it's going 1 2 3 4 then skips 5 and carries on 6 7 8 9 then we include the hundreds as well so it goes 10 and skips 11 and goes 12 13 14 15 16 and skips 17 and goes 18. There is a pattern in this and I followed it through. It does carry on. The only problem is that the first group has only four before skipping one but all the others have five in a set. I can't work out why!

Investigating the multiples
of 24

Patterns:

24	120	216	312
48	144	240	336
72	168	264	360
96	192	288	384

The first thing I noticed was that at the beginning in the tens column it went 24. I then thought that it must go 2,4,6,8 but when I looked I saw that it went 2,4,7. This is weird I thought, so I kept looking at the numbers after 7 It went 9 I then decided instead of just looking at the tens column I would include the hundreds because after 9 it goes 10 when counting in ones. After 9 it goes 12, 14, 16, 19, 21, 24, 26, 28, 31, 33, 36, 38 When you look at the difference between the numbers it goes (By the way I'm counting zero as a multiple now but even if I didn't you would see why the pattern breaks down at the beginning) 2, 2, 3, 2, 3, 2, 2, 3, 2, 3, 2, 2, 3, 2, 3. See? Look at example 1.

E.g. 1

0 (+2) 2 (+2) 4 (+3) 7 (+2) 9 (+3) 12 (+2) 14 (+2) 16 (+3) 19 (+2) 21 (+3) 24 (+2) 26 (+2) 28 (+3) 31 (+2) 33 (+3) 36

These two pieces of work illustrate Clare's discovery of zero as a multiple.

Multiples and angles

If students investigate the total number of degrees in the angles inside a triangle, a quadrilateral, a pentagon, a hexagon, a heptagon, an octagon, a nonagon and a decagon, they will find the sequence of multiples of 180.

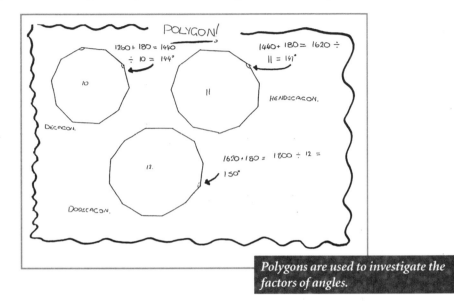

POLYGON!

1260 + 180 = 1440
÷ 10 = 144°

1440 + 180 = 1620 ÷
11 = 141°

10

11

HENDECACON.

DECACON.

12.

1620 + 180 = 1800 ÷ 12 =
150°

DODECACON.

Polygons are used to investigate the factors of angles.

Multiples of eight

The sequence of multiples of eight is introduced by asking students how it might be like the sequence of multiples of four. If the list of multiples of four is on display, some children may be able to use that to generate the sequence of multiples of eight.

When the students have completed their investigations of the multiples of eight the teacher can introduce a diagrammatic method of recording the pattern of reduced multiples. The students have reduced the multiples of eight to produce the following pattern.

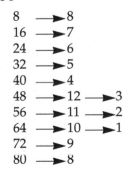

```
8  ──▶8
16 ──▶7
24 ──▶6
32 ──▶5
40 ──▶4
48 ──▶12 ──▶3
56 ──▶11 ──▶2
64 ──▶10 ──▶1
72 ──▶9
80 ──▶8
```

The teacher can supply each student with a template of a nine-clock to trace when carrying out this task.

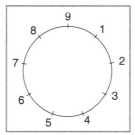

The pattern of reduced multiples is reproduced on the nine-clock by drawing lines from the first number to the next and so on until the first number recurs.

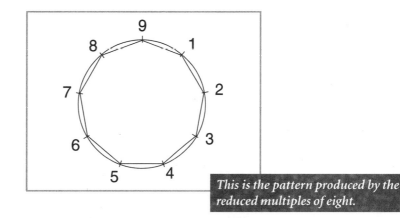

This is the pattern produced by the reduced multiples of eight.

The students can do the same for other sequences of multiples they have studied. They are likely to find relationships between the nine-clocks produced for multiples. For example, the same pattern appears on the clock for the multiples of three and six, for the multiples of four and five, for the multiples of zero and eight and for the multiples of two and seven (that is, pairs of numbers that add together to equal nine). In the case of each pair, the patterns are formed in the opposite directions. Then there are identical clocks for the multiples of nine, eighteen, twenty-seven and so on. Children will make predictions for clock patterns. For instance, what do they think the pattern will be for the multiples of twelve?

Common multiples

By now some students may have noticed that some numbers, such as twenty-four, appear often as multiples. The teacher introduces the term **common multiple** in the context of investigations such as the following.

★ Which multiples are common to both three and four?

It is essential to build students' understanding of terms before they are expected to use them confidently. In the case of the **lowest common multiple**, the students' experiences with concepts and language should focus first on **multiples** and then on **common multiples** before the full term can be clearly understood.

Problems such as the following can provide the context for using the concept of the lowest common multiple.

★ There are several cherries in a bowl. You can work out how many there are if I tell you they can be shared equally between 3 people, between 5 people or between 2 people. What is the least number of cherries that could be in the bowl?

When set the task of finding the lowest common multiple of seven, four and three and to explain why the chosen strategy works, David produced the following piece of work.

Lowest common multiple of 7, 4 and 3

Multiples of 7: 7, 14, 21, 28, 35, 42, 49, 56, 63, 70, 77, 84

Multiples of 4: 4, 8, 12, 16, 20, 24, 28, 32, 36, 40, 44, 48, 52, 56 60, 64, 68, 72, 76, 80, 84

Multiples of 3: 3, 6, 9, 12, 15, 18, 21, 24, 27, 30, 33, 36, 39, 42, 45, 48, 51, 54, 57, 60, 63, 66, 69, 72, 75, 78, 81, 84

84 is the lowest common multiple of 7, 4, 3
This strategy works because it cannot not work.
If you doggedly pursue each list of multiples, then you have to find the lowest common multiple sooner or later. It may not be fast but it's the most reliable.

David explains the strengths and weaknesses of his strategy to define the lowest common multiple.

As David suggests, this strategy is not fast, and it is not the only one. Students can be led to discover a more efficient strategy, as is demonstrated in the following account of a discussion in a Year 5/6 class.

Teacher: How would you find the lowest common multiple of two and six?

That's easy, it's six. I just know it because straight away I can see that six is a multiple of two because it's even.

T: So you don't always have to list the multiples of each number?

Not when they're easy ones.

If it's two and an even number then you can just tell it's the even number.

T: What if you want to find the lowest common multiple of four and twelve?

Twelve, it's twelve. Because twelve is a multiple of four.

I know! If one of the numbers is a multiple of the other then the big number is the lowest common multiple.

T: How would you find the lowest common multiple of two and three?

I think it's six because I can think of the multiples of them but I don't need to write them down. It's easy with some numbers.

If you did the lowest common multiple of two and an odd number, it's double the odd number I think. Yeah, it has to be. Like if it's two and five, the lowest common multiple is ten.

T: Does that always work? Work in your groups to see if that works all the time. Have a look at shortcuts to finding the lowest common multiple of other numbers.

This topic is rich in possibilities for investigations that explore number relationships, while leading to the development of effective strategies for finding lowest common multiples. The class whose discussion is recorded above, later focused on finding the lowest common multiple of two odd numbers. The teacher asked one group to tell her what they had discovered.

We tried the lowest common multiple of three and five and it was fifteen. Then we tried five and eleven and it was fifty-five.

And we thought you could just multiply the two numbers and then you'd get their lowest common multiple.

But when we tried three and nine, it didn't work because we know their lowest common multiple is nine, but three times nine is twenty-seven.

So we did lots more and we found out it works if the biggest number is not a multiple of the smallest number.

Teacher: What if you had to find the lowest common multiple of three odd numbers?

We'll try that next.

Multiplication Strategies

Doubling

Many children initiate work on doubling numbers and this leads to further investigations on multiplication. To introduce doubling, a teacher can begin by writing: 1, 2…

Teacher: What might be next in this number sequence?

Well it could be three.

T: It could be, but not this time.

Four? You could be doubling.

The teacher adds four.

And next could be eight.

Eight is added to the sequence.

Yes, you're doubling. Now it's sixteen. Then thirty-two. Then sixty-four.

The students are set the task of continuing the sequence. They do not use a calculator, but investigate other ways to double numbers, thus providing a valuable, purposeful context for computation practice.

Later, the teacher sets the task of investigating the sequence of numbers generated by starting with three and repeatedly doubling: 3… 6… 12… 24 etc. Another interesting sequence is the sequence generated by starting with five and repeatedly doubling: 5… 10… 20… 40… 80… 160. Note the relationship between this sequence and the binary sequence.

When students work on sequences such as these they will realise there are several different doubling sequences, therefore, the term is appropriate for many. This gives the teacher a good opportunity to introduce the term **binary sequence** to distinguish it from other doubling sequences.

Multiplying by single-digit numbers

As students investigate multiples, they gain familiarity with multiplication facts. Questioning students will reveal what they have learned from their investigation of multiples that relates to multiplication. The following questions focus on the list of multiples of four discussed earlier.

Teacher: Does the list of multiples of four help us work out the answer to this problem that Lina wrote:

★ 8 horses were racing around a racetrack. How many legs were there?

T: Can you use the list to work out what six times four is?

T: If you multiply eighty-eight by four, what would you already know about the answer before you work it out?

To the last question students might suggest the answer would be even, and end in: 0, 2, 4, 6 or 8. These comments indicate an awareness of the characteristics of multiples of four. The teacher then asks students to suggest what the size of the answer might be.

Teacher: Will it be more or less than 100? What digit will it end with? Will it be close to 400? Can you use the list of multiples of four to work out the answer?

To explore multiplication strategies, children are set tasks such as this.

★ Investigate multiplying two-digit numbers by 4. What strategies could you use?

Two children's responses to this task were as follows.

When I did twenty-three times four I said four times twenty is eighty and I kept that in my head and I did four times three and that was twelve so I did eighty plus twelve and that was ninety-two.

First I started with twelve. I doubled it which is twenty-four. Then I doubled it again, forty-eight.

Studying the multiples of six reveals some interesting multiplication relationships.

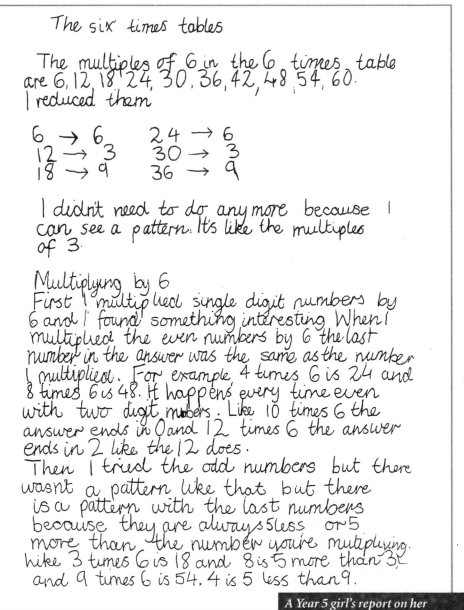

The six times tables

The multiples of 6 in the 6 times table are 6, 12, 18, 24, 30, 36, 42, 48, 54, 60. I reduced them

6 → 6   24 → 6
12 → 3   30 → 3
18 → 9   36 → 9

I didn't need to do any more because I can see a pattern. It's like the multiples of 3.

Multiplying by 6
First I multiplied single digit numbers by 6 and I found something interesting. When I multiplied the even numbers by 6 the last number in the answer was the same as the number I multiplied. For example 4 times 6 is 24 and 8 times 6 is 48. It happens every time even with two digit numbers. Like 10 times 6 the answer ends in 0 and 12 times 6 the answer ends in 2 like the 12 does.
Then I tried the odd numbers but there wasn't a pattern like that but there is a pattern with the last numbers because they are always 5 less or 5 more than the number you're multiplying. Like 3 times 6 is 18 and 8 is 5 more than 3, and 9 times 6 is 54. 4 is 5 less than 9.

A Year 5 girl's report on her investigation of the multiples of six.

The teacher followed these observations by turning students' attention to multiplication strategies.

Teacher: If you were asked to multiply twenty-four by six, what would you predict about the answer?

It would end in four.

T: Right. How would you work out the answer?

You can do six times twenty and six times four and add them together. It's 144.

T: Do you all know how Renee worked that out? Let's write down the steps she took. Renee, what did you do first?

I thought what six times twenty is, that's 120.

The teacher writes 120.

Then I said six times four is twenty-four.

The teacher writes twenty-four.

Then I added them and that's 144.

T: Amanda wrote a problem a couple of weeks ago that I'd like you to work out now in groups. Then each group can write another problem involving multiplying by six to share with the class.

★ There were 253 beetles crawling over my bedroom floor. How many legs was that?

The standard algorithm

Teaching a standard multiplication algorithm is very similar to teaching the standard addition algorithm outlined earlier. As with addition, children are likely to calculate from left to right when allowed to devise their own methods. Aimee reported her method for multiplying a three-digit number by a single-digit number as follows.

First I look at the numbers and say if the numbers were two times 121. I (sort of) did that. I said to myself two times 100 = 200, that's the hundreds covered. Then I said two times twenty is forty, that's the tens covered. I know that two times one is two. Now I've got the answer. The answer is 242.

The teacher introduces the standard multiplication algorithm by asking children to investigate how they could work from right to left. There are many investigation topics that provide multiplication practice.

★ What happens when you multiply numbers ending in 4 by 6?

★ What happens when you multiply a number ending in 13 (e.g. 113, 213) by 6?

★ Investigate what happens when you multiply numbers with zeros on the end (e.g. 80, 800, 8000) by 6.

★ Investigate what happens when you multiply 142 857 by any single digit number up to 7.

A Year 4 boy wrote the following report of his investigation into the topic:

★ What happens when you multiply numbers ending in 4 by 6?

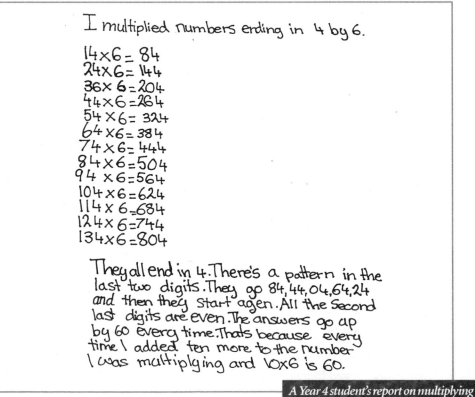

I multiplied numbers ending in 4 by 6.

14 x 6 = 84
24 x 6 = 144
36 x 6 = 204
44 x 6 = 264
54 x 6 = 324
64 x 6 = 384
74 x 6 = 444
84 x 6 = 504
94 x 6 = 564
104 x 6 = 624
114 x 6 = 684
124 x 6 = 744
134 x 6 = 804

They all end in 4. There's a pattern in the last two digits. They go 84, 44, 04, 64, 24 and then they start agen. All the second last digits are even. The answers go up by 60 every time. Thats because every time I added ten more to the number I was multiplying and 10 x 6 is 60.

A Year 4 student's report on multiplying numbers ending in four by six.

Most students will be keen to try several examples when they investigate topics such as the one featured, as they will enjoy the success of being able to do the multiplication and they will be interested in the patterns they produce.

These investigations provide the practice that is needed for students to gain confidence and competence in computation and they provide a purpose for the practice. It is important to explain to students that they should not use a calculator as working through the examples helps them understand why certain patterns occur.

Multiplying by eleven

Exploring the multiples of eleven is an appropriate introduction to multiplying by two-digit numbers. It is a topic that invites extensive investigation and the patterns produced enthuse most students.

Here is an account of a Year 4/5 class investigation into the multiples of eleven. The students worked at their tables and shared their findings as they worked.

Teacher: Let's start with listing a lot of multiples. All of you have a go at making your own list.

They're double digit numbers!

Only up to ninety-nine.

It's easy adding eleven, you just add ten and then one, I could do hundreds of these.

Hey! There's 121 and 242. They're the same backwards and forwards.

T: Numbers that are the same backwards and forwards are called palindromes. Has anyone found any more palindromes in the sequence?

Eleven and twenty-two and thirty-three and the others like that, are they palindromes?

T: Yes, they are.

I bet 484 is the next palindrome.

T: Why's that, Matt?

Because 242 is double 121 and 484 is double 242.

T: *Matt's predicting that 484 will be the next palindrome after 242. Does anyone have another prediction?*

Well it could be 363.

Matt: *Oh yes, it could be... It is 363. Then 484 will be next.*

I've noticed something. The number in the middle is what you get if you add the two numbers on the outside.

T: *That's an interesting comment. Let's stop and have a look at that. We're just looking at the three-digit multiples now. Do the two outside digits always add together to equal the middle digit?*

The students mark the ones on their lists that do not follow this pattern.

11	231	451	671	891
22	242	462	682	902
33	253	473	693	913
44	264	484	704	924
55	275	495	715	935
66	286	506	726	946
77	297	517	737	957
88	308	528	748	968
99	319	539	759	979
110	330	550	770	990
121	341	561	781	
132	352	572	792	
143	363	583	803	
154	374	594	814	
165	385	605	825	
176	396	616	836	
187	407	627	847	
198	418	638	858	
209	429	649	869	
220	440	660	880	

Students discuss the patterns in the sequence of multiples above. The numbers that are underlined are the ones where the two outside digits do not combine to produce the number in the middle. Looking at the three-digit multiples, the first nine do have the two outside digits adding to the middle one, next there is a group of eight, then seven and so on until there is only one (990). In between these groups are groups of numbers where the two outside digits do not add to the middle one, and these groups increase by one each time.

I notice that the ones where it works have the outside numbers matching the number that's multiplied by eleven to get that multiple.

Teacher: What do you mean, Kylie?

The sixteenth multiple is 176. It has the two digits in sixteen on the outside then you add them together to get seven and that's the number in the middle.

T: If we try multiplying a number by eleven we can check that, and we might be able to see why we get that pattern. Let's try the eighteenth multiple. Have a go at multiplying eighteen by eleven. Be ready to talk about the strategies you're using.

It's 198. I counted down my list of multiples until I got to the eighteenth one.

Yes, it's 198. I timesed eighteen by ten and that's 180, then I timesed eighteen by one, that's eighteen so I added 180 and eighteen and I got 198.

T: That's a useful strategy. Let's see how it works for multiplying fourteen by eleven.

That'll be 154.

T: Let's multiply to check. Now, Michael, you thought about eleven times a number being the same as ten times the number plus one times the number. If we imagine eleven bags with fourteen books in each bag, we can work out how many books are in ten of the bags very easily, can't we.

140.

T: Let's write that down. Then we've got one more bag of fourteen books. Let's write that down underneath and we can add the two numbers together.

If the teacher then leads the class through several other examples and records the numbers in the following way, the students may see why they get the results they do.

140	150	160	130	180	170
+14	+15	+16	+13	+18	+17
154	165	176	143	198	187

It is important to set most computations in the context of a problem. If students write the problems, the lesson is more likely to be successful as students will attend more clearly to the concept, be keen to share their own problems and work on the problems of their peers. Their problems will most likely be more inventive than any written by a teacher and they will provide a child's perspective, often with a touch of humour.

Multiplying by numbers greater than eleven

When they are confident with multiplying by eleven, students are set the task of investigating how they could multiply by twelve.

You multiply the number by ten, then you double the number, then you add them.

Teacher: This is like the strategy for multiplying by eleven, isn't it. How is it like that strategy?

For eleven you multiply by ten then by one, and for twelve you multiply by ten then by two.

T: So you multiply by ten then by two and add those two answers.

★ Imagine you earn $15 a month in pocket money. How much would that be in a year? How much would you earn in the first ten months? And how much would you earn in the last two months?

It is important to keep returning to problems in this way, particularly those written by the students themselves, to provide a context for computations. It is very useful to keep a file of problems that the students have written to be used when appropriate.

Through a series of investigations, students transfer their strategy for multiplication by eleven and twelve to multiplication by any two-digit number, and by larger numbers:

★ What happens when you multiply a number ending in 7 by 13?

Kate and Louise in Year 6 wrote the following instructions for multiplication by fourteen.

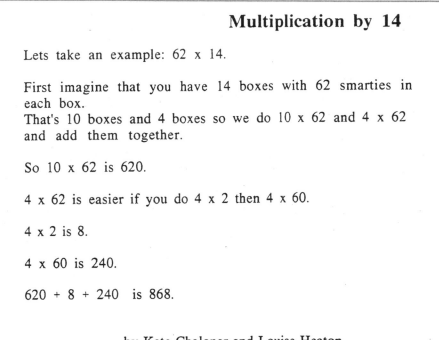

Multiplication by 14

Lets take an example: 62 x 14.

First imagine that you have 14 boxes with 62 smarties in each box.
That's 10 boxes and 4 boxes so we do 10 x 62 and 4 x 62 and add them together.

So 10 x 62 is 620.

4 x 62 is easier if you do 4 x 2 then 4 x 60.

4 x 2 is 8.

4 x 60 is 240.

620 + 8 + 240 is 868.

by Kate Chaloner and Louise Heaton

Kate and Louise's instructions for multiplication by fourteen.

The teacher discusses with students, the value of working out multiplication without using a calculator, helping them realise that written calculation helps them find out why they get particular answers and why certain patterns occur. For instance, the following account by a Year 6 girl demonstrates how she came to understand why numbers ending in three, when multiplied by twelve, produce an answer ending in six with the tens digit odd.

$$13 \times$$
$$\underline{12}$$
$$26$$
$$\underline{130}$$
$$156$$

$$23 \times$$
$$\underline{12}$$
$$46$$
$$\underline{230}$$
$$276$$

There's always a 6 on the end because 3×2 is 6 and the middle number is always odd because you always get an even number of tens in the top row because any number multiplied by 2 is even. And you always get 3 tens in the second row because 10+3 is 30 and the even number in the top row plus 3 is odd.

Written calculation can provide answers for certain patterns.

There are many possible investigations that provide purposeful computation practice while students explore interesting patterns.

★ Investigate multiplying odd numbers by odd numbers, evens by evens and odds by evens.

★ Investigate the squares of the numbers in this sequence: 32, 132, 232, 332, 432...

★ What happens when you multiply a sequence of numbers by the same number such as 11 x 18, 21 x 18, 31 x 18, 41 x 18 and so on?

★ Investigate multiplying numbers comprised only of ones. For example, 11 x 111, 111 x 111, 11 x 1111 etc.

★ What is the largest answer you can reach by using the following symbols once each: 7, 3, 2, ¥, =? To find the answer, students will need to do the following calculations: 73 x 2, 37 x 2, 27 x 3, 72 x 3, 23 x 7 and 32 x7.

★ What happens when a number ending in 4 is multiplied by a number ending in 6?

What happens when a number ending in 4 is multiplied by a number ending in 6?

I know that all the answers will end in 4 because $4 \times 6 = 24$.
I want to find out if there are any other patterns so I will do lots of examples and I will do them in order.

$16 \times$	$26 \times$	$36 \times$	$46 \times$	$56 \times$
14	24	34	44	54
64	104	144	184	224
160	520	1080	1840	2800
224	624	1224	2024	3024

$66 \times$	$76 \times$	$86 \times$	$96 \times$
64	74	84	94
264	304	344	384
3960	5320	6880	8640
4224	5624	7224	9024

Examples, it seems, in which the numbers end in 6 and 4 and that have the same number of tens (example 56 and 54) will finish in 24.

Katherine's report into the multiplication of numbers ending in four by six.

When Katherine shared her findings with the class, the students began to investigate other possibilities such as numbers ending in six and having an even number of tens multiplied by a number ending in four and having an odd number of tens (e.g. forty-six times fourteen).

Multiples of ninety-nine

Students will want to return from time to time to working with sequences of multiples as it is an aspect of mathematics with which they achieve a lot of success. They will suggest topics themselves and like to focus on interesting numbers such as ninety-nine. Generating the list of multiples of ninety-nine provides an opportunity to find shortcut strategies for adding and multiplying ninety-nine.

The multiples of 99:

99	1287	2475	3663
198	1386	2574	3762
297	1485	2673	3861
396	1584	2772	3960
495	1683	2871	4059
594	1782	2970	4158
693	1881	3069	4257
792	1980	3168	4356
891	2079	3267	4455
990	2178	3366	4554
1089	2277	3465	4653
1188	2376	3564	4752

The Patterns:

To start off with until 1188 the two outside numbers are the multiples of nine and the middle number is nine. When you get to 11 x 99 you get 1089. Then comes 12 x 99. If you look closely that is 1188, 18 and 18. That is the second number in the nine times table. We are onto the second group of numbers. For the next 10 numbers 18 appears in the 1st and 3rd numbers: 1_8_. The other two spaces are filled with other multiples of 9 starting at 27. 1287. When you get to 23 x 99 you get 2277. 27 and 27. For the next 8 numbers 27 is in the first and third columns and the multiples pop up again. The 27 group starts at 2079 and actually for the next 10 numbers 27 appears. Another pattern is that the 1 and 3 numbers equal nine when added and the same with the second and fourth. This is because when you reduce the multiples of nine you always get nine! Another pattern is associated with pattern number 1.

As I told you before, you get a repetitive number e.g. 1188. These numbers are on 12x 23x 34x 45x so as you can see the units go up by one and so do the tens! Another pattern is in the tens and units columns, it goes like this: 99 98 97 96 95 94 93 92 91 90 89 88 87 86 85 84 83 82 81 80 79 78 77 76 75 74 73 72 71 70 69 etc. Quite a lot of these patterns are the same as the nines pattern.

Clare's report of the multiples of ninety-nine.

Square Numbers

A study of square numbers will extend children's understanding of multiplication. To introduce the concept of a square number, the teacher should present visual models using materials such as blocks on the floor or squares of card on an overhead projector. The sequence of squares begins as follows.

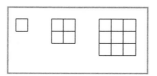

A lesson on square numbers with a Year 4 class continued as follows.

Teacher: What do you think comes next in the sequence?

A bigger square.

A square with four rows with four cubes in each row.

A square with sixteen cubes.

T: Let's record how many blocks make up each of the squares.

A child writes: 1, 4, 9, 16.

T: These numbers have a special name. Can you think what it might be?

Square numbers.

T: Yes, it's fairly easy to see why they're called square numbers.

Let's see what we can find out about square numbers.

The children then worked in groups to continue the sequence of square numbers and search for patterns. They made visual models of square numbers, pasting squares of coloured paper into square formations or printing them using blocks with square or round faces.

The sequence of square numbers goes odd, even, odd, even
and so on.

The final digits form a pattern.
They go 1, 4, 9, 6, 5, 6, 9, 4, 1, 0 and then repeat
Do you see the reverse pattern in this sequence?

The square numbers reduce to make this pattern: 1, 4, 9, 7, 7, 9, 4, 1, 9,
and then repeat.
Do you see the reverse pattern in this sequence?
It's almost the same as the final digits pattern.

The difference between the first two square numbers is 3, then
the difference between the second and third square numbers
is 5 and the differences after that are 7, then 9 and so on with
all the odd numbers.

If the starting number is odd then the square number is odd
and if the starting number is even then the square number is even.

For example, odd numbers: 3 x 3 = 9
                          5 x 5 = 25

           even numbers: 4 x 4 = 16
                        10 x 10 = 100

The observations of the Year 4 class on the sequence of square numbers.

Square number problems

There are many problems which involve square numbers. Some are posed as the students do their initial investigation, while others are set at different times to review square numbers. Some examples of problems involving square numbers follow. Others will appear later in the book.

Fountain problem
Outside the High Court building in Canberra there is a fountain with several fountain heads arranged like this. What is the least number of fountain heads that I need to count to work out the total number of fountain heads in the whole arrangement?

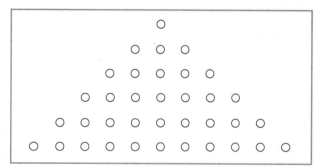

This problem will involve students in an investigation of the arrangement which many students call an **up-and-down staircase**. They will discover that up-and-down staircase numbers are the same as square numbers and, by cutting and rearranging, they will find out why this is so.

Exploring this arrangement of a square number may also lead students to realise that a square number is made up of consecutive odd numbers. In answer to the problem, the students should be able to work out that the least number of fountain heads that needs to be counted is the number of fountain heads in the central column; squaring this number will give the total number.

The following problem is related to square numbers and provides an opportunity for a teacher to focus students on the strategy of working systematically through an investigation of a problem.

Squares within squares problem
How many squares can you find in the diagram below?

The students could discuss this problem as a class and suggest strategies for finding an answer. Together they will find the large square, the nine small squares and the four squares are each comprised of four small squares. Students then label the different size squares they find. They might call them one-ers, two-ers and three-ers. Or they might call them one-layer squares, two-layer squares and three-layer squares.

Next, the teacher uses the labels the students have suggested, along with diagrams, to record the numbers of each.

One-ers	9
Two-ers	4
Three-ers	1

If the students do not notice spontaneously that the square numbers appear above, the teacher can ask them what is special about the numbers of each size square. This should lead them to notice the sequence. The students then work in groups to find how many squares there are in a four-layer and a five-layer version of the square. As they work, they will find the sequence of square numbers continues.

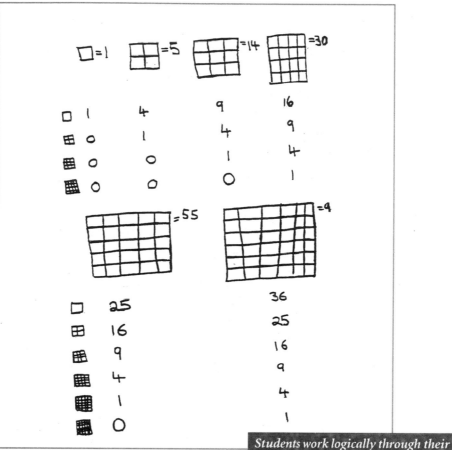

Students work logically through their
investigation of squares within squares.

Outfits problem
Imagine a child with 15 pairs of shorts and 15 T-shirts.
How many different two-piece outfits can the child wear?

The outfits problem leads students to suggest simplifying the problem, by
working with smaller numbers, as a strategy to find the solution.

Most students will begin by drawing the possible combinations of shorts
and T-shirts and will soon find the task arduous. The teacher could then ask
them if they can think of a way to make the problem simpler. The obvious
way, to most students, is to reduce the number of shorts and T-shirts the
child owns (say, three of each). The students may comment about the large
number of each:

No-one would have that many. They must be rich.

Some students may suggest starting by working out how many outfits there would be if the child owned one pair of shorts and fifteen T-shirts. By working with a smaller number of shorts and T-shirts, the students will more easily work out a strategy for solving the problem, usually involving drawing the different outfits. The teacher can suggest they record the answer for the smaller number, then try another number of shorts and T-shirts, and then some more, until a pattern emerges. In this way, the students should find that the answers are all square numbers, and they will be able to work out the answer to the original problem.

Students working on the alternative problem of one pair of shorts and fifteen T-shirts will see there are fifteen possible outfits for one pair of shorts and may suggest that by multiplying the fifteen pairs of shorts in the original problem by the fifteen possible outfits associated with each pair, they will be able to arrive at the answer. By sharing the two strategies, the children will be helped to make the connection between square numbers and multiplying a number by itself.

Square number investigations

Calculator investigations

★ How could you use the calculator to find the square numbers in order from 1 to 100?

★ What is the largest square number you can get on your calculator?

★ What is the 23rd square number?

★ What is the next square number after 6561?

★ Which multiples of 10 are square numbers?

Square roots

The term **square root** is introduced once students have developed the concept. The following investigations use the term **starting number**, one invented by the students in that class to describe the concept of a square root.

★ 441 is a square number. How can you use a calculator to find its starting number?

★ What square number has 26 as Its starting number?

When the students were very familiar with the concept, and comfortable using the term starting number, the teacher introduced the term square root as the one used by mathematicians to mean a starting number. The students were also introduced to the square root symbol and explored the use of the calculator key bearing that symbol.

SQUARE ROOTS

If you want to find a square root on a calculator you push the number then the square root key. For example: if you want the square root of 64 you have to push [6] then [4] and push [√] and the answer should be 8.

* Annette, why did you choose 64 as your example?

Because it's a square number.

* What would happen if you pressed [6] [3] [√]?

You would get 7. something.

Students were introduced to the term square root and its corresponding key on the calculator.

A useful game for memorising square numbers and their square roots is the familiar game of 'Concentration'. It requires a set of twenty cards, ten of them showing the first ten square numbers, and the other ten showing the numbers '1' to '10' (that is, the square roots of the first ten square numbers). The cards are placed face down on a table or floor and players take turns to turn over two cards at a time. If the two cards are a matching pair of a number and its square (for example, '8' and '64') then the player keeps that pair. The aim is to collect more pairs than any other player.

Relating square numbers and triangular numbers

In comparing the sequence of triangular numbers with the sequence of square numbers, students may find the difference between the first terms in each, then the second and so on; in doing so they will find that the triangular number sequence emerges: $1 - 1$ (0), $4 - 3$ (1), $9 - 6$ (3), $16 - 10$ (6), $25 - 15$ (10), etc. Students can explore what happens when any two consecutive triangular numbers are added.

After noting that triangular numbers are formed by adding consecutive numbers beginning from one, students are set the related task of investigating what happens when consecutive even numbers are added, or when consecutive odd numbers (always starting from one) are added. This latter forms the sequence of square numbers.

Investigating squaring odd and even numbers

The following report from a Year 5 girl gives an indication of what can be discovered during work on squaring odd and even numbers.

Squares of odd and even numbers

If you start with an even number and find its square it will also be even and if you start with an odd number and find its square it will also be odd. For example 4^2 is 16 and 5^2 is 25.

The sequence of odd squares goes like this.

1	225
9	289
25	361
49	441
81	529
121	625
169	729

There's a pattern with the final digits. They go 1, 9, 5, 9, 1 and then they do the same again. I found something interesting. It is not possible for a square number to end with 3 or 7.

The sequence of even square numbers goes like this

4
16
36
64
100
144
196
256
324
400
484
576
676

The final digits go 4, 6, 6, 4, 0 and repeat. Square numbers can't end in 2 or 8.

The sequence and patterns of odd and even square numbers as discovered by a Year 5 girl.

When the children in one class shared their findings from this investigation, one student commented that the even square numbers were all multiples of four. The multiples of four up to 400 were listed on display in the classroom and the teacher knew there was another interesting pattern to be found and devised the following questions for discussion.

Teacher: Which multiples of four are square numbers?

The first one is.

T: What strategies could you use to find which other ones are?

We could count down the list until we get to each one. Count down to the next one and it's the fourth one.

T: Can you think of a strategy using a calculator?

You can try different numbers and multiply them by four and see if they are square numbers. It's easier to count them.

T: Could you use division?

Yes you could divide the square numbers by four. Would that work?

T: Who would like to try James's suggestion on a calculator to see if it works?

The teacher had noted that most students were more interested in counting down the list, but a few students were enthusiastic about using a calculator, so provision was made for both methods to be used. The students were fascinated to find that the sequence of square numbers emerged again. The multiples of four that are square are the first, fourth, ninth, sixteenth, twenty-fifth, etc.

Rectangular Numbers

The teacher introduces the topic by asking the students to recall what a square number is, and then asking what a **rectangular number** might be. They may suggest:

A number that can be made into a rectangle.

Using materials such as Unifix cubes, students will investigate the concept and suggest that any number can be a rectangular number as they have defined it, because a row of cubes is a rectangle. While some mathematicians define rectangular numbers differently, the students' definition offers the potential for exploring the concept of factors and is worth pursuing.

When the students realise that all numbers are rectangular, the teacher can explain the interesting aspects of rectangular numbers are that some numbers can be formed into just one rectangle, but others can be formed into more than one rectangle. For instance, five cubes can only be arranged in a single row while six cubes can be arranged in a single row or in two rows of three.

There are many possible investigation topics related to rectangular numbers.

★ Investigate the different rectangular patchwork quilts that can be made from 24 patches.

★ How many different rectangular arrays can be made with 60 Unifix cubes?

★ What numbers less than 50 can only be formed into one rectangle?

★ Investigate the number of rectangles that can be formed for each of the numbers up to 20.

★ Investigate the number of rectangles that can be formed for each of the first 12 multiples of 3.

Factors

The topic of rectangular numbers is a good starting point for introducing **factors**. To ensure students build a sound understanding of the concept of a factor, the teacher can introduce factors in different ways. Already, the students have noted that some numbers appear in many sequences of multiples, and they have found that some numbers can produce more than one rectangle. Another avenue to understanding factors can be used at this stage.

Teacher: The number twenty-four keeps turning up in lists of multiples, doesn't it! Let's look at that number today. Can you count to twenty-four if you count by twos?

Yes: 2, 4, 6, 8, 10, 12, 14, 16, 18, 20, 22, 24.

T: And of course you can count to twenty-four by ones. Let's find all the different ways you can count to twenty-four.

The students will find they can count to twenty-four by: 1, 2, 3, 4, 6, 8, 12 and 24. The students are then set the task of finding another number that can be counted to in many ways; this task will call on a knowledge of commonly occurring multiples and thus build on work the students have already done.

Another avenue is through division. The book by Pat Hutchins, *The Doorbell Rang*, (Penguin [Puffin Books], London 1986), which involves sharing twelve cookies between different numbers of children, is a good focus. The teacher sets the students tasks such as:

★ Work out how many people can share 18 cookies so that each person has the same number.

The results of this investigation can be compared with the different ways of counting to eighteen.

Teacher: Let's have a look at the number of people who can share the eighteen cookies.

1, 2, 3, 6, 9 and 18.

T: Now let's see the different ways we can count to eighteen.

You can count by 1 and by 2 and by 3, by 6, 9 and 18.

They're the same numbers.

T: Those numbers are called the factors of eighteen. There are six factors of eighteen.

Students can investigate the factors of various numbers. They should discuss what strategies they use to find factors and, if students have not already discovered it, the teacher can lead them to the idea that most factors come in pairs, as one student expressed it. These pairs are related to the rectangles that are made from the number so it is important that students keep making rectangles as a basis for investigating factors.

Students' observations during their investigations of factors form the focus of further investigations. The following example is from a Year 5/6 class.

I think even numbers have more factors than odd numbers. Do they?

Teacher: We could investigate that. How could we organise our investigation?

We could try all the numbers up to twenty.

I think we should try some big numbers too.

This next account is from a Year 4 class.

Look! Eighteen's got six factors and nine's got three factors. Ten's got four factors and five's got two factors. The number that's half the big number has half the number of factors.

Teacher: That's an interesting discovery. How many pairs of numbers did you try it with?

Just eighteen and nine, and ten and five.

T: Is that enough examples to be sure you're right?

No. I'll try some more.

T: Well, I think we could ask everyone to have a go at that. Let's start with pairs that have an odd number for the smaller number because I notice that's what you've tried so far. Half of eighteen is an odd number and half of ten is an odd number. What other pairs could we try?

One and two, three and six and seven and fourteen.

T: Are there any other numbers we should try?

Bigger numbers like twenty-five and fifty.

T: And later we can try pairs with the smaller number that is even like twenty-four and twelve.

Linking factors with square numbers

Students are asked to compare the number of factors square numbers have with the number of factors of non-square numbers. They will find that square numbers have an odd number of factors, while other numbers have an even number of factors. By making pictures of all the possible rectangles of a square number, they should be able to work out why this is the case. The following report was produced by a pair of Year 5 girls.

Square numbers & Factors

Square numbers have an odd number of factors and we will show you why. Here are the rectangles you can make with 16 squares (16 is a square number).

4×4   2×8   1×16

The numbers beside the rectangles are the factors. The two long rectangles have two numbers beside them but the square has one number times by itself. So that's why square numbers have an odd number of factors because every square has one of its rectangles that's a square

A comparison of square and non-square numbers and their factors.

Another lesson on factors linking with square numbers is introduced as follows.

The teacher writes for all to see: 1, 10, 100, 1000, 10 000, 100 000 and asks what the next number in the sequence will be. Most students realise it will be 1 000 000.

Teacher: If I asked you how many factors 1 000 000 has, could this sequence help you work out the answer?

There might be a pattern.

T: What sort of pattern?

One might have one factor, then ten might have two factors and 100 might have four factors, and so on. The binary sequence.

T: So if you started by finding out how many factors there are for one, then ten, then 100, you might be able to predict how many factors 1 000 000 has. Let's work on this task today and see what we can find.

The students will be able to find that one has one factor, ten has four factors and 100 has nine factors. They may recognise the sequence of square numbers and predict that 1000 would have sixteen factors. They can check this and finally be able to predict that 1 000 000 has forty-nine factors. Many students are keen to find all forty-nine!

These investigations involve students in building their knowledge of number relationships as they work systematically to find the factors. They can ask themselves questions such as:

★ If 4 is a factor of 1000, can 8 also be a factor? Can 16 be?

★ If 2 is a factor of 1000 can 20 be a factor? Can 200 be a factor?

They will note patterns between pairs of factors, too. If fifty and twenty are factors of 1000, one can be halved and the other doubled to find another pair, twenty-five and forty.

Linking factors with the binary sequence

Investigating the factors of numbers in the binary sequence is a task which generates fascinating patterns. A Year 5/6 class report on this investigation follows.

We worked out the factors of numbers in the binary sequence as far as 64. They go like this:

1: 1
2: 1, 2
3: 1, 2, 4
8: 1, 2, 4, 8
16: 1, 2, 4, 8, 16
32: 1, 2, 4, 8, 16, 32
64: 1, 2, 4, 8, 16, 32, 64

The factors are the binary sequence!

If you add up all the factors for one of the binary numbers the answer is one less than double the binary number.

eg. We added the factors of 8 and we got 1+2+4+8=15 which is one less than 16 and 16 is double 8. You can do the same for all of them. e.g. 64. Add the factors. 1+2+4+8+16+32+64=127 which is one less than 128 and 128 is double 64.

When the factors of numbers in the binary sequence are added together, they equal one less than double the binary number.

Factors and angles

If students investigate the factors of 360, they can relate these to the angle sizes of shapes that tessellate about a point. For instance, equilateral triangles tessellate about a point because their angles are 60 degrees, and sixty is a factor of 360. Students can explore many design possibilities related to this concept.

Introducing prime numbers

Some of the investigations undertaken earlier will make students aware that some numbers can only be arranged in one rectangle; a single row of cubes, and therefore, have only two factors. The teacher can introduce the term **prime number** for numbers that have only two factors.

The term **composite number** would be introduced later, when the students are very familiar with the use of prime number. Introducing two terms at the one time can be confusing. It should be pointed out at this stage that the number one is not a prime number as it has only one factor and prime numbers have two. The children begin to search for, and list, prime numbers. Once they have started this task, they then record the prime numbers found on a chart listing the numbers to 100 in the following format. (The prime numbers are underlined.)

1	2	3	4	5	6
7	8	9	10	11	12
13	14	15	16	17	18
19	20	21	22	23	24
25	26	27	28	29	30
31	32	33	34	35	36
37	38	39	40	41	42
43	44	45	46	47	48
49	50	51	52	53	54
55	56	57	58	59	60
61	62	63	64	65	66
67	68	69	70	71	72
73	74	75	76	77	78
79	80	81	82	83	84
85	86	87	88	89	90
91	92	93	94	95	96
97	98	99	100		

Students can discuss the chart and may be able to conclude that prime numbers are either one more than or one less than a multiple of six (with the exception of the prime numbers two and three, which, as one child noted, are factors of six, making them interesting in this context).

'Maths Party' activity

For this activity, 100 plain round biscuits are arranged in a ten by ten array and iced, the even numbered biscuits in white icing and the odd numbered biscuits in coloured icing. The next step requires a large number of coloured sweets. The students place a yellow sweet on every biscuit, a red sweet on every second biscuit, a green sweet on every third biscuit, etc. Some colours will have to be used more than once. Students are fascinated to find some biscuits have many sweets while some only have one. The sixtieth biscuit has the most, and the teacher can ask the students why they think that is so. Some students will realise it is because the number sixty has the most factors of any number up to 100. They may also note that the prime numbered biscuits are the ones with only two sweets.

In one class, a group of children made a picture of this activity using coloured paper circles for the biscuits and confetti for the lollies. They displayed the picture on the wall and it became a long-term reminder of factors and a reference point for later work.

Measuring Area and Volume

Investigations involving the measurement of area and volume provide opportunities for practising multiplication and applying an understanding of factors. The following topics are examples of appropriate investigations.

★ What strategies could you use to work out how many square centimetres you would need to cover a rectangle measuring 25 cm x 10 cm?

★ How many different rectangles can you draw with an area of 12 cm^2? (The possible ones include: 12 cm x 1 cm, 6 cm x 2 cm, 4 cm x 3 cm and 24 cm x 0.5 cm.)

★ Now that you know how to measure the area of a rectangle, investigate how you might measure the area of a right-angle triangle. How many right-angle triangles can you draw with an area of 18 cm^2?

★ What strategies could you use to work out how many cubic centimetre blocks would fill a box 12 cm long, 6 cm high and 8 cm wide?

★ How many boxes can you design with a volume of 72 cm³?
Choose one of your designs and construct the box. Decorate
your box to show what it might contain.

Cubic Numbers

As students explore space and measurement topics, they will be introduced
to concepts that will initiate work with numbers. For instance, in exploring
the volume of cubes, they will use multiplication and start looking at cubic
numbers. The following example is an account of an investigation of cubic
numbers by a Year 4 class.

Emma had explored square numbers with great interest and when,
shortly afterwards, the class was exploring cubes she asked her teacher if
there was such a thing as a cube number. The teacher suggested she explore
the idea to see if she could answer her own question. Emma, and her friend
Renee, took a tub of Unifix cubes to their table and began making cubes of
various sizes. After some time the teacher asked what they had found. Renee
said:

You can make different cubes with these so we're calling them cube numbers.

Emma was writing in large print on a sheet of paper:

★ Is 10 000 a cube number?

She intended that the written question be displayed for the class to work on,
and the teacher suggested that be the focus of the next day's investigation.
Emma further suggested that the term **cube number** be changed to **cubic
number**, explaining that was the correct term.

On the following day, Emma and Renee pinned up their question for the
class to read. The teacher asked the class to work out what a cubic number
might be, using Unifix cubes or MAB blocks. As they collected their
materials, a few students said that 1000 would be a cubic number because
the MAB thousand is a cube. One boy said:

Well one must be, too, because it's a little cube.

Another student gathered several of the MAB thousands saying:

I'm going to find out what multiples of 1000 are cubes.

The students built cubes with their materials and recorded the number of blocks in each cubic arrangement. No student had enough materials to go beyond a cube of twenty-seven, so they spontaneously formed pairs to share their materials, and a little later joined with other pairs to form larger groups. All the students worked systematically, beginning with the smallest cubic number they could build and increasing each dimension by one with each new cube they constructed. Gradually all the students decided it was an arduous task constructing the cubes and counting the many Unifix cubes, and they turned to calculators in an attempt to make their work easier. The teacher asked them to explain how they were using the calculators.

You go something times something and that makes a square number then you put squares on top of each other to make the cube so you times by the same number again. Like it's three times three for the squares and you've got three squares so it's times by three again.

Yeah, you go something times something times something, six times six times six.

You multiply a square number by its square root!

As the students worked, the teacher sat with groups, in turn challenging them with questions such as:

★ What is the thirteenth cubic number?

★ What is the largest cubic number you can display on your calculator?

★ What is the cubic number after 4096?

★ How could you find cubic numbers without a calculator or blocks?

★ How could you find the cubic root of a number?

Once they had generated a list of cubic numbers in a sequence, the students started writing reports. Two girls worked together to write the following report.

Cubic numbers

A cubic number is a number that can be formed into a cube if you are using blocks that are cubes. For example, you can make a cube with one block and you can make a cube with eight blocks so one and eight are both cubic numbers. Here are some cubic numbers starting from the smallest.

$1 (\to 1), 8 (\to 8), 27 (\to 9), 64 (\to 10 \to 1), 125 (\to 8), 216 (\to 9), 343 (\to 10 \to 1), 512 (\to 8), 729 (\to 18 \to 9), 1\,000 (\to 1)$ we reduced them in the brackets.

The first one is odd then there's an even, then an odd agian then a even agian and it keeps going like that. When you reduce them there's a pattern too, it goes 1, 8, 9 and repeats.

A report detailing the pattern they found when reducing numbers in the cubic number sequence.

James and Ben, working together, produced the following piece of work that began with them recording, in a row, the first eight cubic numbers. The second row records the differences between the consecutive cubic numbers; for example, the difference between eight and one is seven, so seven appears in the second row between one and eight. The following rows record the differences between the numbers in the row above. They explained their process as:

We introduced zero as a cubic number to make the pattern (in the third row) work. It's: 0 x 0 x 0.

0		1		8		27		64		125		216		343
	1		7		19		37		61		91		127	
		6		12		18		24		30		36		
			6		6		6		6		6			

After the students had shared their work, the teacher helped the students recall the symbolism for squaring a number (e.g. 5^2) and asked them to suggest how five cubed might be written (e.g. 5^3) and how: 5 ¥ 5 ¥ 5 ¥ 5 ¥ 5 (5^4) would be written. Then she focused on James and Ben's work. She led the class to discuss including zero in the sequence of cubic numbers as Ben and James had done and asked if this was also appropriate for the sequence of square numbers.

Multiplying Decimals

It is important to return to concrete and visual models as students work with numbers, so they develop a strong understanding of numbers and relationships. If students are working a lot with numbers outside the context of problems, exploring patterns of decimals with calculators for instance, it is vital they balance this work with making models of what they are doing. The following investigations involve students in using coloured paper squares to make patterns that model calculations.

Students can investigate working out the following sequence of numbers by making models of them with coloured paper squares: 1.5^2, 2.5^2, 3.5^2, 4.5^2, 5.5^2, 6.5^2 etc. They can work in groups, each group doing one or two of the models. The model for 3.5^2 is set out below.

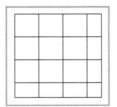

Students can work out the answers to each squared number by counting the squares and fractions of squares. They will find a pattern in the sequence of answers: 2.25, 6.25, 12.25, 20.25, 30.25, 42.25. Students can predict the squares of the next numbers in the sequence and check them with a calculator.

Multiplication and division of decimal numbers occur when solving problems or working with statistical data focused on money and measurement and usually involve the multiplication or division of a decimal number by a whole number. Some students may like to be challenged to find strategies for working calculations where both numbers are decimals.

> Multiplying 6.5 by 3.5
> We estimated the answer would be about
> 24 because it's close to 6×4. We thought it
> looked like 65 × 35, so we did that first
>
>   65 ×
>   35
>   ───
>   325
>   19 50
>   ─────
>   2275
>
> Then we thought the answer would be
> 22.75 because that's close to 24. It
> couldn't be 227.5 or 2275 or 2.275! We
> checked on the calculator and   we
> were right.

A group of Year 6 students wrote this report of an investigation into multiplying decimals.

An interesting topic suggested by one student is the following.

★ What happens when an odd number point five is multiplied by another odd number point five (for example, 3.5 x 5.5) and when an even number point five is multiplied by another even number point five?

Permutations and Factorials

An investigation topic set by a group of Year 4/5 students in the context of multiplying decimals was the following:

★ What is the largest total you can get if you use the numbers 1, 2 and 3 in this arrangement: _._ × _ = ?

This meant students had to work out 1.2×3, 2.1×3, 1.3×2, 3.1×2, 3.2×1 and 2.3×1.

The problem featured is an example of a permutation problem where a specific number of objects have to be arranged in all their possible ways. To build on the concept introduced by the students' problem, the teacher suggested they go on to explore the possible arrangements of the letters A, C and T. The students easily found cat, cta, act, atc, tac, tca.

Next, the teacher asked them to see how many boats they could draw with a hull, a large sail and a small sail, and using three colours, each colour to be used for one item only in each drawing. The students found six possible boats, and some were able to make the connection with the A, C and T task. Then the teacher asked them to add a flag and a fourth colour and they were surprised to find they could now draw twenty-four boats. When asked to find the number of boats with just a hull and a sail and two colours, they came up with two possibilities. The class listed the sequence of numbers they were producing and recognised that with one colour and just a hull on the boat there could be only one drawing. So the sequence began: 1, 2, 6, 24.

The teacher left the sequence on display for several days and asked if the students could predict the next number in the sequence. The students were not able to do so at first but they were interested in trying to work it out over the following days. To assist them, the teacher suggested they investigate how many ways they could arrange five different letters and work out a strategy to make sure they did not miss any possibilities.

Here are the reports of two Year 6 girls who were working on this type of investigation.

Permutations   **by Michelle**

RULES

R 4 2-letter starts

U 4 2-letter starts

L 4 2-letter starts

E 4 2-letter starts

S 4 2-letter starts

5 x 4 = 20

20 x 6 = 120

EXPLANATION

I started listing the words beginning with R then stopped and found an

easier way. I worked out how many words I could with RS at the

beginning. It equalled 6.

I then worked out how many two-letter beginnings there were in

RULES. The answer was 20. I then had to times 20 by 6, the answer is

120. That is the answer to how many words I could make.

I helped Clare with her way of working it out and it was really clever.

You could work it out using 4 or 5 letter beginnings as well.

Michelle's report of permutations using the letters: R, U, L, E, S.

Permutations
  by Clare

How many different permutations are there of the letters CLARE?

Clare

Clrae

Clear

Clrea

Claer

Clera

With this way I can see that it will take ages to work them all out so I will work
out a shorter way....... I can't see any way so I asked my friend Michelle what she
had worked out. I get it and it is along the tracks of what I thought.

I was just going to write Michelle's way when I thought, I want to think of my
own way and I have come up with another way but it is really almost the same. I
will explain it.

Explanation:

What I did first was write out the words beginning with Cl. This was the way
Michelle did it so I thought perhaps I could do it with the first three letters. We
worked out how many 3 letter beginnings there could be, the answer was twelve.
Then we did 5 x 12 because there are five letters in Clare and with each letter
there are twelve possible three letter combinations starting with that letter. Then
we timesed 60 by 2 because there were 2 words we could make with each three
letter beginning. The answer is 120. That's how many permutations for Clare
there would be.

Clare's report of permutations using the letters in her name: C, L, A, R, E.

So the sequence now looked like this: 1, 2, 6, 24, 120. Most students had developed the same strategy as Michelle and in the process of doing so many of them found that multiplication is the basis for the sequence.

You start with one, then to get the next number you times it by two, then you times that by three to get the next number, then you times that by four and so on.

Teacher: So if I asked you how many ways you could arrange six letters could you predict how many there would be?

It's six times 120. 600 … 720!

At this stage the teacher can tell the students they have discovered factorials, explaining that three factorial is written 3! and is calculated by multiplying $1 \times 2 \times 3$. So 3! is six and 4! is $1 \times 2 \times 3 \times 4$ which is twenty-four. Students can explore the sequence of factorials, noting perhaps that after 1! all the numbers are even and from 5! they all end in zero. They can be asked to discuss why this happens.

To follow up Ben and James's work (see page 97) the teacher suggested the students investigate the differences between the numbers in the sequence of squares, and the differences between numbers that were multiplied together four times. The sequence of factorials arises in this context.

The differences between square numbers are taken to two rows and the final row difference is two. 2! = 2

0		1		4		9		16		25		36		49		64
	1		3		5		7		9		11		13		15	
		2		2		2		2		2		2		2		

The sequence of cubic numbers results in three rows to a final difference of six. 3! = 6

The sequence of numbers multiplied together four times results in four rows of differences, with the final difference being twenty-four. 4! = 24

0		1		16		81		256		625		1296		2401
	1		15		65		175		369		671		1105		
		14		50		110		194		302		434			
			36		60		84		108		132				
				24		24		24		24					

Subtraction

Subtraction Contexts

Subtraction is a complex area and teachers need to present a range of subtraction contexts in order for students to develop a full understanding and competency.

Finding differences

In the case of word problems, subtraction is primarily finding the difference between numbers. For example, in each of the following problems, the task is to find the difference between the two numbers.

★ I want to buy a video player that costs $450, but I only have $385. How much more do I need to save?

★ I had $450 and I spent $385 on a CD player. How much should I have left?

★ I took $450 with me when I went shopping and I came home with $385. How much did I spend?

Finding differences can be achieved by taking away or adding on, and children need many opportunities to discuss these two general strategies. To familiarise students with the term **difference**, and to initiate discussion amongst children about their strategies for finding differences, tasks such as the following can be set.

★ What two numbers am I thinking of? They are both less than 40. The difference between the two numbers is 20. They are both multiples of 4. When you reduce the numbers, you get an even reduced number and an odd reduced number. (The answer is 8 and 28.)

★ The difference between two square numbers is 17. What are the numbers? (64 and 81)

Taking away

The other common purpose for subtraction is the investigation of number patterns, which involve subtraction as 'taking away'.

★ What happens when you start with 100 and repeatedly subtract 4 (or any other number)?

★ What happens when you subtract 7 from numbers ending in 3?

Single-digit Subtraction Strategies

Investigating strategies for subtracting numbers up to ten and linking them to adding the same numbers can be attempted by students. For example, if they have a successful strategy for adding nine, can they find a related strategy for subtracting nine? If they think about how they add three, can they find a similar way to subtract three?

Children who add nine by adding ten and subtracting one may subtract nine by subtracting ten and adding one. If they add three by counting on, they might subtract three by counting back. Students work in groups to devise methods to subtract single-digit numbers, with the teacher setting tasks such as:

★ What strategy can you use to subtract a single-digit number from 13? Try 13 − 9, 13 − 8 and 13 − 7 etc.

Subtracting Larger Numbers

As with addition, the teacher uses problems written by the students to introduce the topic of subtracting larger numbers.

Estimation

Estimation is an important first step when subtracting larger numbers and students can discuss the ways they estimate. Two ways to make an effective estimate are: matching final digits and rounding numbers.

Matching final digits

To lead children to use the strategy of matching final digits, they are set tasks such as the following. The various strategies used by the children can then be compared amongst the class.

★ What is a good strategy for estimating the difference between 93 and 44?

When the children explain the strategies they used, someone may say:

Ninety-three is close to ninety-four, and ninety-four take away forty-four is fifty, so the answer will be close to fifty.

If this method is not suggested, the teacher can lead the children to it by asking:

What if I had asked you to estimate the difference between ninety-four and forty-four?

Some children will be able to give the correct answer quite quickly, probably along with an explanation that it is easy to work out such a calculation because the final digits are the same. With occasional oral practice, particularly in the context of solving problems or exploring number patterns, the children will be able to adopt this strategy for estimation.

Rounding

Rounding can also be practised in context. For example, if a problem requires the students to find the difference between eighty-two and thirty-nine, the numbers can be rounded to eighty and forty, and the students can estimate the difference as forty.

From their estimations, some children will quickly reach the correct answer. Taking that step should be encouraged and practised. The potential to move easily from an estimation to the correct answer increases the importance of estimation as a mental computation strategy.

Mental subtraction

Students should be encouraged to use mental subtraction to investigate topics such as the following and later share their strategies with each other.

★ What strategy could you use to subtract multiples of 10, like 20 or 30?

★ Investigate ways to subtract 18 from another number. Can you do it in your head? What about subtracting 29?

★ Investigate what happens when you begin with 1000, and keep subtracting 37. What is a good strategy for subtracting 37?

★ Investigate what happens when you start with 95 and keep subtracting 11. How will you subtract 11 each time?

95
11
——
84

73

6 2

5 1

4 0

3 9

28

17
——
6
——

I kept on subtracting 11

I can see a pattern
it is, the units goes
5, 4, 3, 2, 1 .... and the
tens goes 9, 8, 7, 6, 5...
thats the pattern I see.

One student's report on subtracting multiples of eleven.

Mental subtraction for many students should be accompanied by the use of materials such as MAB blocks and these should always be readily available. Students will not be successful at computation unless they can visualise numbers, and concrete materials help them to do this. A very strong background in mental computation, supported by concrete materials, is essential for success in written computation.

Written subtraction

Students who are confident with mental subtraction are ready to learn written subtraction methods. I have seen many students struggle to learn subtraction algorithms and I believe one of the inhibitors to this learning is the usual link made between using concrete materials and written algorithms. The reason is that the natural way to work with MAB blocks (thinking of the number holistically, from left to right) is not the same as working a written algorithm where you have to think and work from right to left. For example, the natural response to subtracting twenty-seven from fifty-three represented by MAB blocks is to remove two tens first, then do some exchanging to remove the seven.

If a student has a good understanding of subtraction through much mental work, linked with the use of MAB blocks, then they can be set the task of learning about written computation without materials. The task of written computation is just that; working with written symbols. Of course this will only be successful if students are confident and competent with mental calculation. Through using MAB blocks they would have learned about exchanging and they will need to apply the same concept in a written calculation. If they are given the opportunity to transfer their understanding from one form of computation to another, rather than simply practising a technique that has been demonstrated to them, they are very likely to become competent at written subtraction.

Students are supported to devise their own written subtraction methods as a first step in working towards a formal subtraction algorithm. In one class, a group of students developed the following method for subtracting 628 from 694.

Step 1	600	Step 2	90	Step 3	70	Step 4	74
	-600		-20		$+4$		-8
	0		70		74		66

Another group devised the following excellent method.

Step 1: $694 - 600 = 94$
Step 2: $94 - 20 = 74$
Step 3: $74 - 8 = 66$

How did I do it? First I took 1 from eighty-one to make 6 more to make 74 and then I took 30 to make 44.

A student explains his strategy for subtracting 37 from 81.

Students can share their own methods with their peers, and compare them. As a next step, I ask students to devise a written method that works from right to left. This is very difficult for them but focuses their attention well and helps them make sense of the strategy of exchanging.

Teachers should be careful about the concepts they use at this stage. It has been common to approach a task like: thirty-three minus eighteen by saying:

Three take away eight you can't do.

But I have had a student say:

I can, it's minus five.

The standard written subtraction algorithms are difficult for students to understand and use. I like to work with children to build a sense of shared endeavour in reaching an understanding of the written algorithm. I let them know it is a difficult task and I encourage them to discuss what they find difficult about it. I often ask students to work in pairs or small groups to build their understanding. I might set each pair or group the task of working on an example, usually taken from one of their problems. The groups work the example then check the answer on a calculator. If their answer is not the same as the calculator's, the calculation on the calculator can be checked to make sure that is correct, then the students can complete the working out again to discover where and why they went wrong in their written calculation. This is a powerful way to use calculators.

Subtraction Practice through Investigations

Many investigations will give students an opportunity to practise the standard algorithm while exploring interesting patterns. For example, the following work resulted from the topic:

★ What happens when you begin with 286 and keep subtracting 25?

The patterns are...
in the units 6,1,6,1,6!
in the tens 8,6,3,1,8,6,3,1

Patterns in the units and the tens sections were discovered when subtracting multiples of twenty-five.

When the class discussed their work at the end of the investigation, they were able to explain that some of the patterns came about because subtracting twenty-five, four times, is the same as subtracting 100. It is important to give students tasks that enable them to explore such number relationships. Other topics for investigation include:

★ Investigate what happens when you subtract 12 from a number ending in 5 (for example, 45 – 12).

★ What happens when you subtract a number ending in 7 from a number ending in 2?

★ Start with 64 and subtract numbers ending in 8 (e.g. 18, 38). What do you notice?

★ Start with 71 and subtract different numbers. What happens when you subtract from a number ending in 1? Which numbers are the easiest to subtract from a number ending in 1? Which are the hardest?

★ What happens when you subtract a number ending in 25 from a number ending in 26 (e.g. 426 – 225)? What happens when you subtract a number ending in 26 from a number ending in 25 (e.g. 525 – 126)?

★ What do you notice about the answers to the following subtractions?

636363	848484	626262	414141	717171	616161
– 363636	– 484848	– 262626	– 141414	– 171717	– 161616

Try some more like this.

★ Using each of the digits 1, 2, 3 and 4 once only, make pairs of two-digit numbers and find their differences (for example, 43 – 12). Which pair gives the smallest difference and which gives the largest difference?

★ Choose three different digits and form them into a number beginning with the largest digit and finishing with the smallest. Next, write the reverse of this number under the first one and subtract the second number from the first. Reverse the answer and write it underneath, then add it to the answer. For example:

```
   832
 - 238
 -----
   594
 + 495
 -----
  1089
```

Try several other examples. The same can be done with 4 digits, 5 digits and so on to reveal an interesting result.

★ Choose a three-digit number where the final digit is one less than the first digit (say, 362), reverse the number (263) and subtract the second number from the first (362 – 263). Try several examples.

This investigation is followed by investigating three-digit numbers where the first digit is two more than the last, and others where the first digit is three more than the last.

★ Use the bus timetable to work out how long the bus should take to get from school to the furthest bus stop on the school route. Is the time between stops fairly uniform?

★ In a half-hour television show, how much time do the advertisements take, and how much time does the actual show take? Is it the same for all half-hour shows on commercial television?

Negative Numbers

In their subtraction investigations, there are opportunities for students to experience negative numbers. Not all students in primary school will be able to understand the concept of a negative number, but many will be fascinated by it.

The following account of an investigation in a Year 4/5 class demonstrates the different levels of operation within a class, with several of the students exploring negative numbers. The set task was:

★ Investigate what happens when you start with the number 1689 and keep subtracting 250.

All the students began by writing 1689, repeatedly subtracting 250 and recording the answers. Then they branched off in different directions, according to their level of interest and understanding.

Some students used a written algorithm to work out the sequence of numbers.

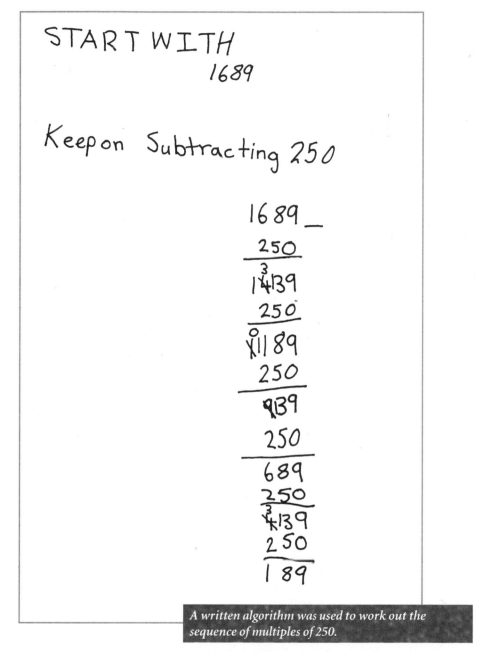

STA RT WITH
1689

Keep on Subtracting 250

16 89 ‾
 250
̇‾
1̂439
 250̇
‾
0̂11 89
 250
‾
9̂139
 250
‾
 689
 250
‾
3̂139
 2 50
‾
1 89

A written algorithm was used to work out the
sequence of multiples of 250.

As they worked, these students were practising the subtraction algorithm
and reporting the following patterns.

All the answers end in nine.

The answers end in eighty-nine, thirty-nine, eighty-nine, thirty-nine and so on.

If you take off 250 four times, it's like taking off 1000, so you get down to 689.

Some of the students went on to try repeatedly subtracting 250 from different starting numbers.

$$1689 -$$
$$250$$
$$\overline{1439} -$$
$$250$$
$$\overline{1189} -$$
$$250$$
$$\overline{939} -$$
$$250$$
$$\overline{689} -$$
$$250$$
$$\overline{439}$$
$$250 -$$
$$\overline{189} -$$

$$1428$$
$$- 250$$
$$\overline{1178}$$
$$- 250$$
$$\overline{928}$$
$$250$$
$$\overline{678}$$
$$-250$$
$$\overline{428}$$
$$- 250$$
$$\overline{178}$$

Different starting numbers for multiples of 250 were introduced by Raabia.

Some students worked mentally, and many continued the sequence into negative numbers, using calculators at this stage.

As they worked, many students set themselves challenges. One boy worked out how to continue the sequence into negative numbers without using a calculator.

1689	−4311	−10061	−15811	−21311
1439	−4561	−10311	−16061	−21561
1189	−4811	−10561	−16311	−21811
939	−5061	−10811	−16561	−22061
689	−5311	−11061	−16811	−22311
439	−5561	−11311	−17061	−22561
189	−5811	−11561	−17311	−22811
−61	−6061	−11811	−17561	−23061
−311	−6311	−12061	−17811	−23311
−561	−6561	−12311	−18061	−2356
−811	−6811	−12561	−18311	−2381
−1061	−7061	−12811	−18561	−2406
−1311	−7311	−13061	−18811	−2431
−1561	−7561	−13311	−19061	−2456
−1811	−7811	−13561	−19311	−2481
−2061	−8061	−13811	−19561	−2506
−2311	−8311	−14061	−19811	−25311
−2561	−8561	−14311	−20061	−2556
−2811	−8811	−14561	−20311	−2581
−3061	−9061	−14811	−20561	−2606
−3311	−9311	−15061	−20811	−2631
−3561	−9561	−15311	−21061	−2656
−3811	−9811	−15561		−2681
−4061				

Nick's list of the multiples of 250 continues into negative numbers.

Another student altered the task to follow his own interest, starting with 1 000 000 and repeatedly subtracting 250, noting many patterns as he progressed. Several students were interested that in the sequence of numbers, the positive numbers ended in nine, while the negative numbers ended in one. They tried starting with other numbers and after a while were able to predict what would be the final digits of the numbers in any sequence. As Aaron explained:

If you add the last digit of the positive number to the last digit of the negative number it'll be ten.

Aaron

1689	1276	1000	1423	1238
1439	1 026	750	1173	988
1189	776	500	923	738
939	526	250	673	488
689	276	0	423	238
439	26	-250	173	- 12
189	-224	-500	-77	- 262
-61	-474	-750	-327	-512
-311	-724	-1000	-577	-762
-561	-974		-827	
-811	-1224		-1077	
-1061	1474		- 1327	
-1311	1 724			
	1974			
	- 2224			

Aaron listed five starting numbers to begin his investigation.

Susan looked at the final two digits of the numbers and said:

In the first list, the plus numbers end in eighty-nine and thirty-nine, and the minus numbers end in sixty-one and eleven. You can plus eighty-nine and eleven and you get 100, and you can plus thirty-nine and sixty-one and you get 100.

Subtracting Decimals

Students do not often write problems involving decimals, so their teacher can ask them specifically to do so. This will reveal what students know about decimals, as well as providing a stock of problems to share with the class.

Investigations involving measurement and money can provide purposeful subtraction of decimals.

★ What is the difference in height between the tallest and shortest boys in our class? Is the difference similar for the tallest and shortest girls?

★ What happens when you subtract $1.75 from $6.15?, $6.25?, $6.35?, $6.45?, $6.55? and from $6.65?

Pyramid Numbers

If the class has explored pyramids, the following question can be posed:

★ What type of pyramid can be made with Unifix cubes?
The answer is, a square-based pyramid.

One way to introduce the topic of pyramid numbers is to present students with the following sequence: 650, 506, 385, 285, 204, 140, 91, 55, 30 and ask them to find the last three numbers in the sequence. As the numbers decrease, most students will use subtraction to search for a pattern. They should find that the difference between consecutive numbers is a square number, and that if they continue to subtract square numbers in turn, the sequence will be completed with the numbers: 14, 5 and 1.

After this introduction, the students can construct pyramids with Unifix cubes or similar blocks and explore the sequence of pyramid numbers.

Division

Division Contexts

Fractions

Once students have begun working with problems involving fractions and in this way gained some familiarity with commonly occurring fractions, they can focus their investigations on fractions. The initial investigations should help students understand the concept of a fraction.

A good introductory investigation of fractions is to generate a sequence of numbers by starting with any number and repeatedly halving. Different starting numbers produce some interesting results.

$$64, 32, 16, 8, 4, 2, 1, \frac{1}{2}, \frac{1}{4}, \frac{1}{8} \ldots$$
$$100, 50, 25, 12\frac{1}{2}, 6\frac{1}{4}, 3\frac{1}{8} \ldots$$
$$88, 44, 22, 11, 5\frac{1}{2}, 2\frac{3}{4} \ldots$$

Another useful introductory investigation, which helps build a concept of a fraction, is to find as many numbers as possible between two whole numbers (say, three and four) and order them. Some students will include decimals such as 3.5 and others will include fractions such as $3\frac{1}{2}$.

Investigation topics focusing on fractions include the following.

★ Investigate halving even numbers, halving odd numbers.

★ Investigate quartering even numbers.

★ Investigate halving each of the numbers in the sequence of multiples of 8.

★ Find a third of each of the numbers in the sequence of multiples of 9.

★ How can you use a calculator to find a third of a number, and two-thirds of a number?

★ Continue the following number sequence and then find a third of each of the numbers: 1, 4, 7, 10, 13… Make a model or picture to show why you got the answers you did.

Quotition division

Quotition division involves sharing a number of objects into a specified number of groups and working out how many there are in each group, for instance, sharing twenty books between five people.

If dividing a large number, it is best to develop a quotition strategy. For instance, if dividing 564 by four, students develop an algorithm that allows them to proceed step by step, sharing out the hundreds, the tens and the ones.

Partition division

Partition division involves working out how many groups of a specific size there are in a number of objects, for instance, how many twos there are in thirty-eight.

When dividing by a fraction it is useful to apply partition division. For instance, if asked to divide eight by a half, it makes more sense to think in terms of how many halves there are in eight ($8 \div \frac{1}{2}$ can be read as: *eight how many halves?*). Some students become very interested in challenging each other with tasks such as dividing a half by an eighth or dividing a fifth by a tenth.

Percentages

A percentage is a form of expression of a fraction. The key task when working with percentages is to convert the percentage to a fraction. Children should be assisted to become familiar with commonly occurring percentages and their meaning, through problems they pose themselves.

Multiplication Tables

Knowledge of the multiplication tables is essential to success in division. Students will gain some familiarity and confidence with multiplication facts as they investigate sequences of multiples and solve multiplication problems.

To learn multiplication facts, students must have access to charts of tables, lists of multiples, lists of factors and sequences of numbers. The teacher should refer often to these lists, using them to solve problems, basing investigations on them and giving short oral or written tests.

Testing children regularly is one way to help them learn the multiplication table facts. If students are allowed to refer to lists or charts on the wall when being tested, they will have a greater number of correct answers and will feel better about themselves. Until students have committed the multiplication facts to memory, they need to be able to use the charts quickly and effectively, and testing them with the charts for reference helps them do so.

Division Strategies

Dividing by single-digit numbers

When students work on division problems they should begin by using the strategies they have developed themselves. Some strategies will be very similar to the standard algorithm as students will often work from left to right.

To guide students towards using the standard algorithm, a teacher can begin by setting sequences of numbers to be divided by two. For example, the following sequence: 2, 20, 200, 2000. Or: 66, 666, 6666, 66 666. The answers can be worked out mentally and recorded in the following way.

$$2\overline{)2}^{\,1} \qquad 2\overline{)20}^{\,10} \qquad 2\overline{)200}^{\,100} \qquad 2\overline{)2000}^{\,1000}$$

At this stage it is useful to divide numbers containing all even digits. As students work on several examples of such sequences, they will note the relationship between the single digits in the answer and in the number being divided. (They do not need to use the formal terms, **quotient** and **dividend**, yet.)

Dealing with odd digits can be introduced in the following way.

Teacher: Let's look at this problem that James wrote.

★ I bought a giant box of smarties and it had 883 smarties in it. How many do I get if I share them with my brother?

T: Could you use the division strategy that we've been investigating?

Yes, can I do it?

T: Yes, Amanda, come and show us on the board how you would write it out.

Amanda writes $2\overline{)883}$.

Teacher: Before you start to work it out, can anyone tell us if it is possible to share 883 smarties equally between two people?

It's an odd number so there'll be one left.

You could cut it in half, but that's hard to do with a smartie. James could have the extra one because he bought them.

T: You're right, there will be one left. OK, Amanda, can you explain what you do as you work out the answer on the board? Listen to Amanda and see if you would work it out the same way.

The students go on to investigate further examples containing odd digits in other positions. They will find it helpful to work in small groups to share their ideas. Then the groups can compare their methods for working with odd digits.

Later the teacher can model the standard method. For most students this will be reinforcing the method they have developed themselves. A model of this strategy can be displayed for later reference.

Students increase their understanding and competence in dividing numbers by two by investigating topics such as the following.

★ What happens when you divide a number ending in 6 by 2?

We investigated what happens when we divide numbers ending in 6 by 2. We did lots of examples.

$$2\overline{)16}\;^{8} \qquad 2\overline{)26}\;^{13}\quad 2\overline{)36}\;^{18}\quad 2\overline{)46}\;^{23}\quad 2\overline{)56}\;^{28}\quad 2\overline{)66}\;^{33}\quad 2\overline{)76}\;^{38}\quad 2\overline{)86}\;^{43}\quad 2\overline{)96}\;^{48}$$

$$2\overline{)106}\;^{53}$$

The answer always ends in 3 or 8. That's because 6 divided by 2 is 3 and 16 divided by 2 is 8. We noticed that when you divide a number ending in 6 by 2 the answer ends in 3 if the tens digit is even and the answer ends in 8 if the tens digit is odd

A Year 4/5 group report of division of numbers by two.

The next focus is division by a single digit other than two, say three. It begins by a review of the three times table and follows the process outlined above for division by two. An appropriate investigation topic is:

★ What happens if you divide a number ending in 9 by 3? Other topics can be set which allow students to practise the division algorithm while they investigate patterns.

★ What happens when you divide an even number by 6? (If there is a remainder, it is 2 or 4.)

★ Investigate what happens when you choose a three-digit number with all digits the same, add the digits and divide the original number by the sum of the digits.

★ What happens when you divide a number with a 0 in it by 2? What if the 0 is the last digit? What if the 0 follows an even digit as in 608? What if it follows an odd digit as in 504?

★ What happens when an odd number is divided by 6?

> When you divide an odd number by 6 you will always have a remainder ~~with~~ which is odd and below 6. This is because multiples of six are even numbers, and if you divide by 6 a number that is two or four different to a multiple of six your remainder will be two or four. If you divide by 6 numbers that are one or three different from a multiple of six (which, incidentally, are odd numbers) your remainder will be 1, 3 or 5.

One student wrote this account of dividing a number by six.

Another avenue for investigations involving division is to divide the numbers in a sequence by a specific number.

★ Investigate dividing the numbers in this sequence by 3: 11, 21, 31, 41, 51…

Joel, in Year 6, noting that 121 is divisible by eleven, posed the following question for his class:

★ Are the numbers in this sequence of palindromes divisible by 11: 121, 12321, 1234321, 123454321, 12345654321, 1234567654321, 123456787654321, 12345678987654321?
   (Alternate ones are, and their answers are also palindromes.)

Yet another focus for division is the following type of problem:

★ Which five consecutive numbers add to 1820?

A review of the multiples of nine, focusing particularly on the fact that they reduce to nine, can lead a teacher to pose this question:

★ Can all numbers that reduce to 9 be divided by 9 with no remainder?

Students can investigate this by dividing by nine, several numbers like 111 111 111 and 3213 where the digits reduce to nine.

One Year 5/6 class was investigating dividing by nine when Brendon wrote this algorithm for the class to work on: $9\overline{)999\,999\,999}$. Everyone said that was 'too easy' so I suggested to Brendon that he change two of the digits. He wrote $9\overline{)994\,999\,599}$. The class found the answer of 110 555 511 interesting and I then changed the same two digits in the original dividend to produce $9\overline{)996\,999\,399}$. When this number was divided by nine it gave the answer $110\,777\,711$. The children were again fascinated by the answer and started looking at why the pattern occurred. I asked if someone else could change the same two digits to produce an answer with a similar pattern. Amelia wrote $9\overline{)992\,999\,799}$. Next I asked if someone could come up with the dividend which would give the answer $110\,444\,411$.

One pair of children wanted to create algorithms which would give a palindromic answer. They arrived at the following sequence of numbers which were to be divided by nine: $919\,809, 929\,709, 939\,609, 949\,509, 959\,409, 969\,309, 979\,209, 989\,109$.

Making sense of division answers

As students solve problems, they always have to ensure an answer makes sense, both in terms of the size of the answer and the way the answer is expressed. With problems involving division with a remainder, there is a particular need to express that remainder appropriately. Sometimes it will simply be left as a remainder and sometimes it can be expressed as a fraction. Sometimes a further step needs to be taken, as in the case of the following problem.

★ There are 117 students and teachers going on our camp next week; how many people will travel on each of the 2 buses?

Hopefully no student will give the answer fifty-eight and one remainder, nor that $58\frac{1}{2}$ people travel on each bus.

In one classroom where problem posing was not featured, but where the teacher displayed problems around the room, two girls wrote the following problem on a poster for the class to solve. They titled it, *Big Maths Problem*.

| Big maths problem.

There were 215 Sheep and We Wanted them to be rounded off in to 40 Sheep yards?

Can you Solve the problem?

Some problems are displayed on a poster for the class to solve.

It did indeed become a big maths problem as it allowed the teacher to introduce the concept of division answers making sense. The girls who wrote the problem had thought the answer was 5.375 which they had produced on a calculator.

Making sense of calculator answers to division

When students use calculators to find answers to division problems, they will sometimes arrive at an answer with a decimal point, and when they calculate mentally or use a written algorithm, their answers will sometimes have remainders. Teachers have to guide students to make sense of these two different forms of answers. If students are in the habit of doing division in the context of problems, the concept of a remainder will make sense to them. They will often question the decimal remainder in a calculator answer.

<u>1000</u>

1000 is just 1000 ones.
½ of 1000 is 500.
¼ of 1000 is 250.
⅛ of 1000 is 125.
⅓ of 1000 is 333.3333
⅕ of 1000 is 200.
⅙ of 1000 is 166.66666
⅐ of 1000 is 142.85714
⅑ of 1000 is 111.11111
The square root of 1000 is
31.522776

Matthew

Matthew's report detailing decimal remainders and their equivalent fractions.

The teacher can present a series of problems which have answers with a remainder that can be divided up itself. For instance, if sharing five sandwiches between two children, each child can have two whole sandwiches and the sandwich that is left can be halved, giving each child two and a half sandwiches in total. The same problems can be solved with a calculator and the answer compared to the answer arrived at mentally. When the students record the pairs of answers they will notice patterns. If the answer is something and a half, the calculator will say something point five, and when the answer is something and a quarter, the calculator will say something point two five.

Divisibility

Divisibility by five and ten

To introduce the concept of divisibility, a review of the multiples of ten, noting that zero is the final digit in each case, can be introduced. Similarly, students can review the multiples of five and discuss the fact that the final digit is either zero or five. Students should also be guided to note that all numbers ending in zero or five are included on the list of multiples.

One teacher began a lesson on divisibility by drawing a line down the centre of the whiteboard and asking children to call out any numbers between one and 100 and observe if, and where, the teacher was recording them. She wrote those that were multiples of five on the left hand side of the board and those that were multiples of two on the other side. Other numbers were rejected. The children were able to suggest that the ones on the left hand side were multiples of five and the others were multiples of two. The teacher asked the children to explain how they had worked that out, and their explanations centred on divisibility.

They're all ending in zero or five so that means they are multiples of five.

And those ones are all even, so they can be divided by two, so they're multiples of two.

A list of several numbers, some of them multiples of five and others not, was written by the teacher and the students were asked to suggest which ones are able to be divided by five with nothing remaining. Students can be asked to explain how they can tell whether or not a number is able to be divided by five without leaving a remainder. The teacher can use the term **divisible by five**. A poster to display some of the multiples of five could be designed by students, titled: *These numbers are divisible by five* to model the terminology. An alternative title is: *A number is divisible by five if its final digit is zero or five.*

Divisibility by other single-digit numbers

Students can go on to investigate divisibility further, providing purposeful practice in division.

Numbers whose digits add to a multiple of three are divisible by three (e.g. 276 is divisible by three because its digits add to fifteen which is a multiple of three). Numbers whose last two digits are a multiple of four are divisible by four (e.g. 644 is divisible by four because the last two digits are a multiple of four). Even numbers whose digits add to a multiple of three are divisible by six, and a number is divisible by nine if its digits reduce to nine.

I want to see how you can tell which numbers are divisible by 6. So I will write down the multiples of 6 because they are the numbers divisible by 6.

6, 12, 18, 24, 30, 36, 42, 48, 54, 60, 66, 72, 78, 84, 90, 96, 102, 108, 114, 120.

They're all even but if you think an even number is divisible by 6 you're wrong, not all the even numbers are in there e.g. 2 is missing and so is 4 and 8 and 10 and lots more

Ms Skinner said to look at the numbers that are divisible by 3 so I did. I noticed every second multiple of 3 is a multiple of 6. In fact they're the ones that are even look. 3, 6, 9, 12, 15, 18. So I think you can tell if a number is divisible by 6 if it is even and if its digits add up to a multiple of 3. I'll show some examples. 114 is even and 1+1+4=6 (6 is a multiple of 3) 78 is even and 7+8=15 (15 is a multiple of 3 too.)

This report details numbers divisible by six written by Kathy in Year 6.

Divisibility by eleven

Studying a list of the multiples of eleven can prompt students to suggest how to tell whether or not a number is divisible by eleven. A pattern for divisibility by eleven is difficult for students to discover, so the teacher can put the following hypothesis for them to test.

★ Look at the number 34 952. We can say that: 3, 9 and 2 are in odd-numbered places because they are the digits in the first, third and fifth places, 4 and 5 are in even-numbered places because they are in the second and fourth places. A number is divisible by eleven if the digits in the even-numbered places add to the same total as the digits in the odd-numbered places, or if the difference between the totals is a multiple of eleven. That is, in the example of 27 863 which is divisible by eleven, the digits in the even-numbered places are 7 and 6 and they add to thirteen, and the digits in the odd-numbered places are: 2, 8 and 3 and they add to thirteen as well.

Divisibility by twelve

The following series of tasks leads students to explore divisibility by twelve.

★ Can you find some numbers that are divisible by both 3 and 4?

Students should discuss how they went about finding these numbers, and most would have listed several multiples of each and found multiples that were common to both lists.

★ Find some four-digit multiples of both 3 and 4.

Before embarking on this task, students can discuss whether it is appropriate to continue with the strategy of listing multiples and they may realise the enormity of the task. The teacher can ask them to review what they know about divisibility by three and four, and perhaps apply this knowledge. A group of Year 5/6 students had the following discussion with their teacher about the multiples of three and four.

Teacher: Let's look at what you know about four-digit multiples of four. Our list is up here on the wall. Do you remember what makes a number divisible by four?

Its last two digits are a multiple of four.

We could just list the multiples of three and see which ones end in a multiple of four.

T: Yes, you could. But perhaps you know something about numbers that are divisible by three that would make the task easier too. What do you remember about numbers that are divisible by three?

The digits add up to a number that's a multiple of three.

T: *Right, so can you combine that information with what you know about multiples of four?*

We could write down some multiples of four with four digits then we can add up the digits to see if they add up to a multiple of three.

Or we can write down the last two digits and add them up then make sure we write down two digits in front of them that make all the digits add up to a multiple of three.

After the students have worked in groups on this second task, they can be set the final task.

★ The numbers you have listed are divisible by 3 and by 4. They are also divisible by four other numbers. What are these numbers?

The students may already have noted that the numbers are divisible by twelve because, as they responded to the first task, many would have noted that the multiples that are common to both three and four are the multiples of twelve. Now they will be able to discover the numbers are also divisible by one, two and six. Some students will conclude that the multiples of any number are divisible by the factors of that number.

Division with Decimals

Students will meet decimals when using calculators, particularly when investigating division and square roots. A group of Year 4 students reported on their work with square roots as follows.

> If you press 256 on a calculator and then press the square root button 16 would come up on the screen. you can do that with any number. sometimes you don't get a whole number, you get a number with a decimal point. If you press a square number then the square root button you get a whole number.

A report into square roots by Year 4 students.

Linking fractions and decimals

Students can be set the task of investigating the decimal equivalents of known fractions such as: $\frac{1}{2}$, $\frac{1}{4}$, and $\frac{1}{3}$. This is a difficult task which is made easier if students work in groups. The following is an account of a discussion between a teacher and a group of Year 6 girls on converting fractions to decimals.

Teacher: How did you go in your group today? Did it make the work any easier than if you did it on your own?

Rebecca: It was much better in the group. Neroli had a really good idea and that helped me because I didn't know what to do.

T: What was your idea, Neroli?

Neroli: Well, I know a half is 0.5 and a quarter is 0.25 and I thought that twenty-five is half of fifty and 0.5 is the same as 0.50. So I thought if we had to find what an eighth is it would be half of 0.25 and we put zero on that and we got 0.250 and we halved that and got 0.125 so that's probably an eighth.

Katherine: It looked right to me. Then I had an idea for how we could check it because Neroli didn't know if it was right. I said if we work out on the calculator a problem where we know the answer is an eighth then we can see what the calculator says an eighth is. So we went 0.5 times 0.25, we thought that was how you'd do half of a quarter, and we got 0.125!

The connection between fractions and decimals can be reinforced by referring back to the halving sequences produced when the students investigated fractions; converting the fractions to decimals, so that the first sequence: 64, 32, 16, 8, 4, 2, 1, $\frac{1}{2}$, $\frac{1}{4}$, $\frac{1}{8}$, becomes 64, 32, 16, 8, 4, 2, 1, 0.5, 0.25, 0.125.

To introduce the technique of converting a fraction to a decimal by dividing the numerator by the denominator, one teacher conducted the following discussion with a Year 4/5 class. Each student had a calculator with them.

Teacher: Let's look at the symbol for a half. Who can describe it?

It's a line with a one on top and a two underneath.

T: Now what about a quarter?

It's got a line in the middle and one on top and four under.

T: Why do you think half has a two below the line and a quarter has a four below the line?

When you cut something in half you cut it into two parts and when you cut it into quarters you cut it into four parts.

T: Why is there a one on top?

You've got one thing to cut up into halves or quarters.

It means one half or one quarter. If it was a three on top of the four it means three quarters.

T: OK, that's two meanings for the one above the line. Lets look at Steven's suggestion; you've got one thing to cut into halves or quarters. You're talking about dividing it aren't you, when you say cutting it up? Say you've got one thing and you want to divide it into two, how would you work that out on a calculator?

You'd press one, then divided by, then two.

T: Try that on your calculator and see what you get.

I've got 0.5.

T: Now what would you try for a quarter?

One divided by four.

That's 0.25. That's an easy way to get decimals.

T: How do you think you'd find what three quarters is as a decimal?

Would you do three divided by four?

T: What do you all think of that suggestion?

We could try it and see.

In another Year 4 class, the starting point for this work was based on a piece of work one of the students had done while engaging in free exploration with a calculator.

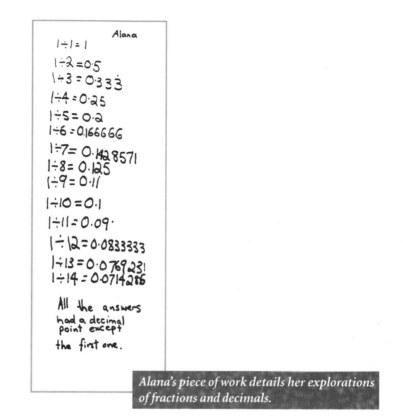

Alana
$1 \div 1 = 1$
$1 \div 2 = 0.5$
$1 \div 3 = 0.33\dot{3}$
$1 \div 4 = 0.25$
$1 \div 5 = 0.2$
$1 \div 6 = 0.166666$
$1 \div 7 = 0.1428571$
$1 \div 8 = 0.125$
$1 \div 9 = 0.11$
$1 \div 10 = 0.1$
$1 \div 11 = 0.09.$
$1 \div 12 = 0.0833333$
$1 \div 13 = 0.0769231$
$1 \div 14 = 0.0714285$

All the answers had a decimal point except the first one.

Alana's piece of work details her explorations of fractions and decimals.

There are some interesting investigations that can be carried out with this strategy. For instance, converting the sequence of sevenths to decimals produces a particularly interesting pattern.

Converting sevenths to decimals

$1/7 = 0.1428571$
$2/7 = 0.2857142$
$3/7 = 0.4285714$
$4/7 = 0.5714285$
$5/7 = 0.7142857$
$6/7 = 0.8571428$
$7/7 = 1$

The pattern in this sequence is that the numbers after the decimal point are the same sequence, but start in a different place each time. Imagining the numbers as a ring helps. The last and the first digit is repeated.

Katherine, in Year 6, described this pattern when converting a sequence of sevenths.

An alternative approach to the sequence of sevenths is to ask students to work out the first five, then predict what six sevenths is. One of the purposes of exploring patterns is to enable students to make predictions.

Students can convert any sequence of fractions, and can return to familiar numbers. One Year 6 girl converted the sequence of eighteenths to decimals and went as far as forty eighteenths, delighting in the strings of repeated numbers that she discovered. The repeating pattern meant that one eighteenth, nineteen eighteenths and thirty seven eighteenths all had .0555555 after the decimal point. Eva converted ninths, then eighteenths, and said:

I'm doing twenty sevenths next, then thirty sixths and other multiples of nine.

Eva

$$\frac{1}{18} = 0.0555555 \qquad \frac{12}{18} = 0.6666666$$

$$\frac{2}{18} = 0.1111111 \qquad \frac{13}{18} = 0.7222222$$

$$\frac{3}{18} = 0.1666666 \qquad \frac{14}{18} = 0.7777777$$

$$\frac{4}{18} = 0.2222222 \qquad \frac{15}{18} = 0.8333333$$

$$\frac{5}{18} = 0.2777777 \qquad \frac{16}{18} = 0.8888888$$

$$\frac{6}{18} = 0.3333333 \qquad \frac{17}{18} = 0.9444444$$

$$\frac{7}{18} = 0.3888888 \qquad \frac{18}{18} = 1$$

$$\frac{8}{18} = 0.4444444 \qquad \frac{19}{18} = 1.0555555$$

$$\frac{9}{18} = 0.5 \qquad \frac{20}{18} = 1.1111111$$

$$\frac{10}{18} = 0.5555555 \qquad \frac{21}{18} = 1.1666666$$

$$\frac{11}{18} = 0.6111111$$

Eva's sequence of eighteenths to decimals.

Why do some decimals repeat infinitely?

To understand why some decimals repeat infinitely, it is useful for students to apply a written strategy to the conversion of fractions to decimals.

Teacher: What is the strategy you use to convert a fraction to a decimal?

We divide the top number by the bottom number.

T: *And you use a calculator. Could you do it without a calculator?*

Probably.

T: *Let's try converting a half to 0.5 with a written division strategy. Who'll write it on the board? Thanks, Taufa.*

Taufa writes $2\overline{)1}$

Teacher: Now what can we do next?

You can't do anything, the number's not long enough.

T: *There is a way to make the number longer. Think about decimals.*

But you can't put zeros on the end because then the number is ten or a hundred, it's not one any more.

T: *What if you put a decimal point somewhere?*

Could you put it after the one and then put a zero?

T: *Let's try that and see what it looks like.*

Taufa adds a decimal point and a zero.

That looks like ten but it's not because it's got a decimal point in the middle. I think it's one, one point zero.

Yeah, that's one, I think it's one. (Several others agree.)

Teacher: You're right. That's another way to write one. Now try to divide it, Taufa.

Taufa puts zero above the one, a decimal point above the decimal point in the dividend, and carries the one over to the zero. She writes five above the zero and is happy with the outcome.

Hey, that works!

The teacher can now ask students to use the written strategy to investigate the decimal equivalents of one third, one sixth and two thirds. They will develop a good understanding of why some decimals continue repeating.

When you divide one by three you keep adding zeros after the decimal point and you get three into ten goes three and one left over. That makes another ten when you add another zero and it keeps going exactly like that.

At this stage, too, the teacher can show students the symbolism for repeating decimals. A further topic for investigation is:

★ Which fractions produce repeating decimals?

One group of students drew on their knowledge of multiples to hypothesise that fractions where the denominator is a multiple of three will produce repeating decimals.

Percentages

Investigations can focus on the relationship between fractions, decimals and percentages. These investigations are most effective when conducted by a group so children can pool their knowledge and ideas.

★ In your group talk about where you have seen or heard percentages. What do you think percentages mean?

★ What does your group think these percentages mean: 100% 50%, 25%, 75%, 1%, 10%?

★ 25% is another way of saying a quarter. For example, if a quarter of the people in our class ride a bike to school, we can also say that 25% of the people in our class ride a bike to school. See if your group can explain why 25% is equivalent to a quarter.

Investigations can also focus on percentage contexts.

★ Using catalogues, investigate what a 20% sale in a toy shop would offer customers.

Percentage calculation devices

When one class surveyed the litter in their school playground their teacher set them the task of showing other classes some of the litter statistics. The class analysed 300 items of litter found on one day and noted that plastic items were the most plentiful. The teacher asked the children to show how the amount of plastic litter compared to the amount of other litter. One pair of boys used a pie graph which they cut into a disc overlaid with a smaller disc showing percentages.

Of 300 pieces of litter there were 208 plastic items. The boys matched approximately where 208 items would be on the large disc to the percentage on the smaller disc and concluded that almost seventy-five per cent of the litter was plastic. They explained to the class how the larger disc could be replaced by other discs with different numbers of things on them. For example, if one day they found only 200 pieces of litter in the playground the markers on the larger disc would be 0/200, 150, 100 and 50.

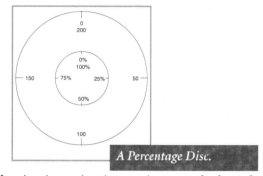

A Percentage Disc.

The teacher set the following investigation topics once the boys had made their Percentage Disc.

★ Make your own Percentage Disc and investigate calculating some percentages.

★ Can you make a Percentage Disc that will help you find 20% of a number? Can you make a Percentage Disc that will help you find $33\frac{1}{3}$% of a number?

★ A calculator can also be used to calculate percentages. Investigate how you can use a calculator to do so.

★ Can you invent a different device for calculating percentages using strips of card?

As a result of the last topic, the children invented a Percentage Strip which looks like this.

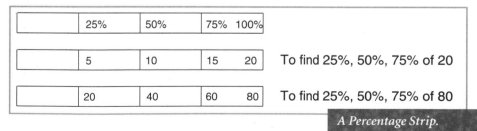

A Percentage Strip.

Conclusion

Computation is best learned in a classroom rich in mathematics, where students explore a range of mathematical ideas and make calculations purposefully. Let me conclude by describing one such classroom, a large room with sixty students and two teachers.

There is a lot of mathematics on display. There are problems; the students' own problems, others that the two teachers have posted, two problems cut from a magazine and brought into class by one eager student. There are challenges that teachers or students have written up:

★ How is rain measured?

★ What is the largest number you can write using 1, 2 and 3, each number once only. (The answer is NOT 321!)

★ What number can you multiply by 5 to give an answer that is less than 5?

★ Investigate the different ways you can draw a right-angle. Which is the most accurate?

★ Can you learn the 13 times table? What strategies can you use to learn it?

Student work is on display. For example, as an outcome of one recent investigation, there is a chart listing the multiples of thirty-seven, recorded as follows:

37	370	703
74	407	740
111	444	777
148	481	814
185	518	851
222	555	888
259	592	925
296	629	962
333	666	999

A caption at the bottom of the chart invites readers to find a pattern across each row. A question added to the chart asks:

★ How can you add 37 in your head?

There is a poster declaring Adriana's hypothesis about a candle clock made with a tapering candle.

> If you make a candle clock with a candle that starts off thin at the top and gets fatter as it goes down, the lines that mark off every 10 minutes will be closer together as they go down the candle.

Paintings and collage pictures that the students created show famous mathematicians such as Maria Agnesi and Benjamin Franklin. There are lists of numbers compiled by students in their investigations, now used for reference in other investigations: the multiples of four and a list of square numbers (with illustrations) are two examples. There are multiplication tables charts. There are visual models of numbers such as a huge display in the hallway outside the classroom of the 'Duke of York's 10 000 men' made by drawing some of the men and multiple-photocopying them, to which some children added figures to produce a task based on the 'Where's Wally' books: Where's the Duke? Where's the Duchess? Where's the Duke's golden sword?

The displays are 'living' displays as they are added to as the students discover more patterns or as the teachers add written questions to extend the ideas presented. Students see their work valued, which enhances both their self esteem and interest in mathematics, and hence their confidence in working with numbers. They also see that their work is done for a purpose, it is 'real' work.

It is notable that the displays cover a wide range of topics. Mathematics teaching is traditionally focused on one topic at a time, but a full understanding of mathematical concepts can only be reached if there is transfer between topics. Transferring in this way enables students to apply the skills and knowledge they are learning, provides purposeful revision of topics and it is more likely that each student will find something of particular interest to them. Talking about mathematics is important to developing familiarity with mathematical language and symbolism.

There are many concrete materials for computation, geometry and measurement, a class set of calculators and books of mathematical information including a few different mathematics dictionaries. The atmosphere in the classroom is one of excitement as the students write problems and explore mathematical topics. Today they are investigating the different right-angle triangles they can draw with an area of twelve square centimetres. Most of them are drawing triangles with a base and height that are factors of twenty-four: e.g. a base of 6 cm and a height of 4 cm. Some of them have moved onto drawing a triangle with a base of 48 cm and a height of 0.5 cm, and two are drawing one with a 16 cm base and 1.5 cm height. The students are talking together, sharing strategies, helping others and commending one another's efforts.

The teachers are moving amongst the children, asking them to talk about the strategies they are using to work out the possible triangles. One group needs more assistance from a teacher. One of the teachers sits with the group and helps them work through their difficulty; they do not understand how to work out the area of a triangle. The teacher asks them if they remember how to work out the area of a rectangle, drawing a rectangle with measurements written along the sides as she talks. The teacher helps the students discuss how they could work out the area and they demonstrate a good understanding of the method. The teacher then asks them how they could cut the rectangle into two triangles. They all see this quickly and one of them cuts the rectangle along a diagonal. The teacher says:

Tell me what you know about the area of each of the triangles.

The students realise that the area of each of the triangles is half the area of the rectangle, and they go on to suggest they could make some rectangles with an area of 24cm^2 and cut them in half to get triangles with an area of 12cm^2. This group is working at a more concrete level than others in the class, but they are still led by the teacher to work out their own strategies for solving a problem.

Open investigation tasks allow all students to work at their own levels while enabling them to feel part of the class, and thus members of a 'community of learners'. The teachers reinforce this when the classes gather together at the end of the lesson. The teacher asks the group to make a poster displaying their work and explain to the others the method they used. The rest of the class discuss why the method the group used was successful, and this reinforces the relationship of the areas of rectangles and right-angle triangles. It is vital to keep returning to concrete and visual models of mathematical ideas to ensure students understand what they are doing.

The teachers involve the students in evaluations of their own progress and of the mathematics program. They ask them questions focusing on different aspects of mathematics. Examples of these questions follow.

By involving the students in evaluation the teachers are demonstrating how much they value the input of the students into the mathematics program. Note that the last question is one which encourages students to suggest topics for further investigation. The key to the success of this approach to mathematics teaching is to engage the students in directing most of the work; posing problems to be solved and suggesting topics to be investigated. Several of the questions target the way students work; 'working mathematically' is as essential to success in mathematics as is developing computation skills.

When students are empowered to pose problems, set investigation topics and evaluate their own performance, when their teachers show they value their ideas and share their enthusiasm and when their teachers set high expectations for them, they will make progress as mathematicians. They will become skilled in computation, learn an abundance of mathematical facts and terms and discuss mathematical ideas with enthusiasm.

Mathematics in this classroom is lively and loved. For these students, it is as natural to chat about mathematical topics as it is to share personal news with friends and teachers.

Posing Questions in View of the Mathematics Teaching Principles

Posing questions:

- How are the questions you are posing now, different from the ones you posed at the beginning of the year?
- Are we covering many different types of questions?
- Is it important to pose different types of questions?

Solving questions:

- Are you finding new ways to solve questions?
- How are you working together to solve questions?
- What do you do if you are stuck on a question?

Investigating:

- What has been your favourite investigation so far?
- What are you learning as you do the investigations?
- Do you find it helpful to work together on investigations?

Communication:

- When you talk with others do you know enough words to explain your ideas?
- Do you find it useful to use diagrams sometimes when you explain your ideas? What sorts of diagrams?

Computation:

- Is it important to learn about fractions? Why?
- Are you improving the accuracy of your mental calculations?
- When do you use a calculator?
- How important is estimation?

Space:

- Is it interesting to investigate shapes?
- Are you finding ways to get better at drawing shapes?

Statistics:

- How do you collect statistics?
- Is it important to be able to work out averages?

Measurement:

- How many different measurement devices have you used?
- Can you think of any investigations we might do that involve measuring liquids?